nifty notes

on
Hugh Leonard's
Home Before Night

by
Aoife O'Driscoll

FOR LEAVING CERTIFICATE
ORDINARY AND HIGHER LEVEL

educate.ie

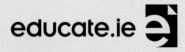

PUBLISHED BY:
Educate.ie
Walsh Educational Books Ltd
Castleisland, Co. Kerry, Ireland
www.educate.ie

EDITOR:
Adam Brophy

DESIGN:
The Design Gang, Tralee

PRINTED AND BOUND BY:
Walsh Colour Print, Castleisland

IMAGES –
O'Connell St, Dublin, page 12: courtesy of Irish Photo Archive; recruitment poster page 45: courtesy of Óglaigh na hÉireann/Irish Defence Forces; other images courtesy of BigStock and Stockbyte/Getty.

The author and publisher have made every effort to trace all copyright holders. If any have been overlooked we would be happy to make the necessary arrangements at the first opportunity.

ISBN: 978-1-908507-88-4

Acknowledgements

I would like to thank everyone at Educate.ie for their help and support, particularly Adam Brophy for his wonderfully constructive advice, patience and encouragement during the writing process. I would also like to thank Janette Condon for her practical and helpful suggestions, Síofra Ní Thuairisg and Jane Rogers for their editorial input, Peter Malone for overseeing the work, and the design team for creating such a visually pleasing book.

Dedication

This book is dedicated to my father, Ger McCarthy, with endless thanks and gratitude.

Aoife O'Driscoll

CONTENTS

Introduction   7

The Scoop   8

1   Historical Background, Summary and Analysis   13

2   Character Analysis   53

3   The Single Text   85

4   The Comparative Study   111

Glossary   162

INTRODUCTION

Whether you are studying *Home Before Night* as a Single Text or as part of your Comparative Study, you will find notes to help you in this book.

Here you will find a detailed summary and analysis of the plot, as well as in-depth character sketches, notes on each of the comparative modes for Ordinary Level and Higher Level, and a step-by-step guide (including sample answers) on how to approach this novel as a Single Text.

Raised on songs and stories,
    heroes of renown,
The passing tales and glories,
    that once was Dublin town,
The hallowed halls and houses,
    the haunting children's rhymes,
That once was Dublin city,
    in the rare oul times.

Ring a ring a rosie as the light declines,
I remember Dublin city in the rare oul times.

~ Pete St John (The Rare Oul Times)

the scoop

Title

Home Before Night is an autobiographical novel by one of Ireland's most prolific writers, Hugh Leonard (1926–2009). The title refers to the closing pages of the book. The author is remembering a time when he was seven or eight and hurrying home before nightfall. To him, home was a place of security, love and warmth, where his parents would be waiting anxiously for his safe return.

Setting

Dalkey, Dublin

Time

The author looks back on his childhood in Dublin in the thirties and forties. He also briefly recounts some of his parents' experiences during the War of Independence and the Irish Civil War. This was a time of great change in Ireland, politically and socially.

Plot summary

Born Jack Byrne, the author is adopted in 1926 by Nick and Margaret Keyes, a working-class couple living in Dalkey. His father, a kindly optimistic man, works as a gardener for the Jacob family near by. Money is tight and the family lives in a small, two-

Hugh Leonard

HOME BEFORE NIGHT

room cottage during Jack's early childhood. They are surrounded by a close community of family and friends.

Jack longs to escape the restrictive confines of his poor background, the stifling affection of his doting parents and the stigma of his illegitimacy. He is delighted when he wins a scholarship to Presentation College because he believes it will be a fresh start and will give him the opportunity to reinvent himself. However, he is bitterly disappointed by the reality: his mother tells the principal the story of his adoption and the other boys spot Jack's shabbily dressed father accompanying him to school. Jack spends four miserable years in secondary school and does not stay on to sit the Leaving Certificate.

Leisure activities for Jack and his teenage friends centre on the seafront and the cinema. They lose themselves in the exploits of their on-screen heroes and wish for the day that they too might have a chance to lead exciting lives.

Six months after he leaves school, Jack joins the civil service. He does not want to do so but is pushed into the job by his mother, who is impressed by the pay and the promise of a pension. Jack loathes his new job and is intimidated by his boss, the intelligent but witheringly critical Mr Drumm. Mr Drumm initially takes Jack under his wing, but later – suddenly and quite inexplicably – falls out with him and makes it his business to ignore or humiliate

Jack at every opportunity.

Jack has always wanted to be a writer but it is not until he goes to see his first play, shortly after joining the civil service, that he is fired up sufficiently to make that dream a reality. He begins to act in and write plays, and after fourteen years becomes successful enough to resign from the job he detests. He moves to England with his wife and child. While he is away, his mother dies and his father becomes senile. He refuses to go to London to live with Jack and eventually dies, two years after his wife.

Two years later, in 1970, Jack comes back to Ireland to live. Having succeeded in escaping, he is now happy to return on his own terms. He is at last in a position to look back on his upbringing with affectionate nostalgia.

The chapters in this novel alternate between first and third person narration. This allows the author to show us both a child's innocent view of the world and an adult's keener understanding of the events in his life. There are more detailed notes on this at the beginning of the Literary Genre section of the notes on the Comparative Study.

Themes

The novel centres on Jack's relationship with his family. He loves his parents and appreciates all they do for him, but he longs to escape the poverty of his upbringing and make a better life for himself.

Doyle family tree

Grandfather Doyle – Grandmother Doyle

(died in 1926 – the year Jack was born)

Sonny	Mary	Christine	Margaret
married	*never*	*married*	*married*
Kate Fortune	*married*	**John Bennett**	**Nicholas Keyes**

——————————— ADOPTED ———————————

Jack Keyes Byrne
the author

Jack
the dog

pen name
Hugh Leonard
1926 - 2009

Historical background, summary and analysis

Changing times in Ireland

The War of Independence (January 1919 to July 1921)

The War of Independence began in 1919. Members of the Irish Republican Army (IRA) waged a guerrilla war against the Royal Irish Constabulary (RIC) and the British forces in Ireland. A truce was agreed in July 1921 and a series of talks began which led to the Anglo-Irish Treaty, signed in December 1921. This treaty allowed for most of Ireland to be self-governing but for six counties in Northern Ireland to remain under British rule. The twenty-six southern counties were called the Irish Free State.

The Black and Tans

During the War of Independence many Irishmen resigned from the RIC, the national police force at the time. The RIC had already been under attack from the Irish Republican Brotherhood (IRB) and the IRA

Carrying out a search; Black and Tans, Dalkey, 1920

for a number of years, and the combination of low morale resulting from these attacks and the defection of those who preferred to join the Irish fight for independence led to a significant drop in RIC numbers. The Black and Tans were mostly ex-British army recruits drafted into the RIC in 1920 and 1921 to help the RIC keep control. Many of the Black and Tans were veterans of World War I who had returned to Britain to find no jobs and few prospects. They answered a British government advertisement looking for men to 'face a rough and dangerous task' in Ireland. Lacking the control and discipline of the army, the Black and Tans soon became notorious for their violence against the Irish population. Their nickname – the Black and Tans – derived from their makeshift uniforms, which were usually a mixture of army khaki and dark police uniforms.

The Civil War (June 1922 to May 1923)

In early 1922, British forces began to pull out of Ireland. The Irish people were split between those who supported the Anglo-Irish Treaty and the Free State, and the republicans who thought that all of Ireland

Michael Collins played a major role in the campaign against British rule and the subsequent Civil War. His life story is the subject of director Neil Jordan's 1996 film, Michael Collins, *with Liam Neeson in the title role*

© WARNER BROS. PICTURES 1996

should be free from British rule. A bitter conflict ensued, with many deaths on both sides, before the Free State forces won the war in May 1923.

The Catholic Church supported the Free State forces and said that Anti-Treaty fighters would be excommunicated. This meant that they could not take part in religious sacraments, were not entitled to a church burial and, in the eyes of many, would lose any chance of going to heaven. This was a serious threat in a country where the vast majority of the population were strict Catholics. In *Home Before Night*, Jack's father is anti-British and pro-republican. Naturally, he disagrees with the Catholic Church's stance on excommunicating republican fighters. Because of this, he is angry and embarrassed when Father Creedon, a clergyman and therefore an enemy of sorts, takes him to task for not teaching Jack his prayers. This is also one of the reasons why he supports Hitler during World War II.

Éamon de Valera kept the Irish Free State out of World War II

The Emergency

'The Emergency' was a term coined by the Irish government to refer to its official position during World War II. Ireland was a neutral country during this war, but declared a state of emergency when war broke out in Europe in 1939.

Why is this historical perspective important?

Jack's parents married in 1905 and adopted Jack in 1926. During this time, they lived through several political changes in Ireland. Jack himself lived through what was known in Ireland as 'The Emergency'. When you read the text, take note of references to the Black and Tans, Jack's father's coolness towards the Catholic Church after the Civil War, and the changes in daily life during World War II. All of these events shape Jack's understanding of the world around him.

Chapter 1

The opening chapter of the book is written in the first person and provides us with an introduction to the Doyles, Jack's mother's family. Jack's grandmother, his uncle Sonny and his aunt Mary share a tiny two-roomed cottage. Jack's grandfather died in 1926, the year Jack was born. He and Jack's grandmother had four children: Sonny, Mary, Christine and Margaret, Jack's mother. Sonny and Mary are the only two children left at home. Margaret married Jack's father in 1905 and Christine (Aunt Chris) married John Bennett.

Jack's grandmother (Mrs Doyle) is described in unflattering terms. She is vastly overweight, unpleasant, a dreadful cook, and insistent that everyone knows when she is suffering from ill health. She easily intimidates those around her, particularly Sonny's fiancée, Kate Fortune, a tall, plain, nervous woman. Mrs Doyle hates Kate and only allows her into the tiny cottage at Christmas. Sonny and Kate's engagement lasts thirty years and they finally marry when Mrs Doyle dies. Kate has a job in the Dargle Laundry, while Sonny has never worked at all. He spends his days at the pub, the labour exchange or the betting office. He is a difficult man, filled with anger and resentment and, like all the Doyles, quick to take offence and make an enemy of anyone he feels has done him wrong. Sonny is convinced that people go out of their way to treat him unfairly.

The other occupant of the cottage is Jack's aunt, Mary. Known locally as 'Mad Mary', she is a large, shapeless woman with the mental age of a seven-year-old. Her mother dotes on her and believes her to be angelic, but young Jack is not so convinced of Mary's saintliness, mainly because of her habit of hurting him when nobody is looking.

An incident from Jack's childhood shows how cunning Mary can be. She steals £2 from her mother and, although she has never been further than the local shop on her own, she manages to leave the house without telling anyone and spends the day at a funfair. Her disappearance causes great alarm; her brother Sonny becomes convinced that she has been taken by a sexual predator. Jack's father tries to reason with him, but to no avail. Sonny goes to the pub, where he broods on the matter. After a few pints, his suspicions fall on Mr Finnerty, a respected, religious man who lives near by. He decides to confront Mr Finnerty and, together with a small crowd from the pub, heads for Mr Finnerty's house. He runs out of steam when he finds the door locked and the lights out, and although he threatens to throw a brick through the window, he doesn't actually do so. The crowd becomes bored and restless and at that moment a policeman arrives on the scene. Spurred into action by this sight, Sonny rushes into Mr Finnerty's back garden, grabs the struts of a small windmill used to generate extra electricity for the house, and manages to knock it down. Nobody is more surprised than Sonny by this outcome. The windmill falls onto Mr Finnerty's conservatory, causing substantial damage. Sonny is arrested and taken away by the policeman, and seems to feel nonetheless that this is yet another instance of the world ganging up against him.

Mary arrives home safely, having cleverly kept aside just enough money for the tram fare, and is unmoved by her mother's anger. Sonny is kept in jail for a week and ordered to pay Mr Finnerty for the damage to his house and windmill. He pays small instalments for a time, but never pays off the full amount.

Jack's aunt Chris is the success of the family. She has always been ambitious for a better life, and because she dresses well and speaks in a refined, mannerly way she is able to find a job with a Dublin milliner rather than as a maid or a cleaner. She makes new friends and begins to move in a more elevated social circle, eventually meeting and marrying a civil servant called John Bennett, a well-dressed, polite man who treats Chris with courtesy and devotion.

John Bennett's introduction to his future wife's family is not an auspicious one. Mrs Doyle insists on cooking for him, Mary makes a great fuss of him, and Sonny mocks his baldness. However, despite being made violently ill by the dreadful, greasy fry he is served by Mrs Doyle, John is not deterred and he and Chris marry. It is not until after their marriage that Chris learns that John's nickname in the civil service is 'Curser Bennett' because of his habit of swearing very volubly, particularly when he has had a few drinks. On discovering this, she soon puts paid to this single fault.

The Bennetts keep to themselves and live a sedate, genteel life. Chris and John are childless, and the first chapter ends with the rather startling revelation that none of the Doyles of Chris's generation had children – including the author's mother.

KEY QUESTIONS

- Is our introduction to Jack's family positive or negative or a mixture of both?

- Although many of the incidents described in the first chapter took place before the author was born, he describes them in vivid detail. A good example of this is the passage in which he describes Chris and John's courtship. Read this section of the novel again. Do the descriptions of the characters' feelings and the use of dialogue make the author's family come to life for the reader?

- What is the effect of the startling ending to this first chapter?

WRITING TASK

- Write the diary entry you think Chris might have written after her first date with John.

Chapter 2

The second chapter is written in the third person and centres on young Jack's complex relationship with his parents, particularly his mother. When she has drink taken she becomes emotional and difficult. One evening, on a cruise around Howth, Jack's mother tells the young boy that if he is naughty his birth mother will come to take him away. She frightens him with this tale and it is several years before he realises that his mother only told him this story because she was drunk.

On the cruise, Jack's mother dances with a strange man, and Jack senses that his father is jealous. He is a peace-loving man but he does have a temper, especially if he feels his family is under threat. Jack remembers that when he was bitten by a dog, his father was so shocked and upset on seeing his son's bandaged face that he flew into a rage.

This evening, Jack and his father do their best to cope with his mother's rapidly changing moods. As they are getting off the boat, Jack's mother stumbles. Instantly, she turns on the man behind her, accusing him of having pushed her. The man is bewildered but soon becomes angry when she continues to accuse and insult him. Jack waits on the quay as his father joins his mother and takes her side against the other man, while at the same time trying to reason with his wife. Jack is embarrassed and upset by the scene his parents are creating, and a passing woman with a young family takes pity on him. She gives him money for sweets and attempts to remonstrate with Jack's parents when they finally get off the boat. Her words are lost, however, as Jack's father, not even pausing in his stride, scoops up his son and quickly marches his family away. There is a note of admiration in the way Jack describes his father sweeping him along in this decisive and rather dashing fashion.

As the family boards the train back to Dalkey, Jack's father does his best to soothe his wife and she listens patiently while he waxes lyrical about how happy and fortunate they are as a family. As his father talks, Jack wonders how long it will take before today's scene fades from people's minds and before he can show his face in public again. It is only August, so he reckons that he should be safe to go out in Dublin again by Christmas. He loses himself in happy memories of visits to Santa and lunches out, but then the woman and her family who had tried to comfort him earlier that evening appear in his vision and recognise him. His daydream is ruined.

Suddenly, Jack's mother begins to chat to two young women sitting

> Jack is embarrassed and upset by the scene his parents are creating, and a passing woman with a young family takes pity on him

close by. She is charm itself and all seems to be going well until one of the girls notices Jack reading his comic. Jack's mother becomes irritated when Jack remains silent in the face of the girls' comments and she grabs the comic from him. It tears as she pulls it and one of the girls expresses dismay. Instantly, Jack's mother's mood changes again. She glares at Jack and tells the girls that he is an ungrateful boy who does not appreciate the fact that she adopted him when his own mother didn't want him. The girls seem to realise that Jack's mother is drunk and she, in turn, thinks that they are mocking her. She begins to shout abuse at them and the girls hurriedly leave the train at the next station, even though, Jack suspects, it is not their stop. The train moves on and Jack holds back his tears until he is safely home.

KEY QUESTIONS

- What do we learn about Jack's mother and father in this chapter?

- What words would you use to describe Jack's emotions on this family day out?

- Read the section in *Home Before Night* in which Jack's mother has an argument with the man on the gangplank. Is there any humour in the way this incident is described?

- This chapter is written in the third person; the events are described from the point of view of young Jack. Does this narrative technique make you more sympathetic towards the young boy?

WRITING TASK

- Imagine you are one of the girls on the train. Write the letter you would send to a friend, describing your meeting with Jack's family.

Chapter 3

Jack's father works as a gardener for the Jacob family. The hours are long and the pay is low, but he holds the Jacobs in high esteem. Jack's mother is less impressed and believes her husband's employers could be more generous. When Mr Jacob dies, Jack's mother is worried that the house might be sold, but the widowed Mrs Jacob chooses to remain there even though she is in poor health. Jack's father returns to the house every evening and, with the help of the family's female chauffeur, carries Mrs Jacob upstairs on a special chair. The driver does not work on Saturdays, so it falls to the fifteen-year-old Jack to assist his father in carrying the heavy, elderly lady to her bedroom on those days. As Jack is thin, not particularly strong and prone to fainting, he dreads this task and he is relieved when a full-time nurse is eventually engaged and his services are no longer required. His payment for all his work is an old, mildewed copy of the collected plays of Shakespeare.

> it falls to the fifteen-year-old Jack to assist his father in carrying the heavy, elderly lady to her bedroom

When Mrs Jacob dies, Jack's mother is hopeful that her husband will receive a lump sum of £100 along with his pension. Instead, the Jacobs' daughter presents him with a cheque for only £25 and a bizarre gift of some wire spectacles that had been fused into a twisted mass in the fires following the San Francisco earthquake of 1906. Mr Jacob had found the tangle of burnt wire in the shell of a jewellery shop and had brought it home as a souvenir. Jack's father is touched by the gift and decides, in his typically optimistic fashion, that it is valuable. His wife is more realistic and far less thrilled, particularly because she cannot pawn the lump of charred metal.

The Jacobs' house, Enderley, is sold and the new owners employ Jack's father. He is required to act as caretaker in the weeks before the new family moves in and he returns from his first night alone in the house in an odd mood. This continues for the two weeks of his caretaking, and on the final night he asks Jack to sleep in the house with him. Jack agrees and is horrified to hear footsteps on the stairs and doors opening after he and his father have gone to bed. It seems that Enderley is haunted, which terrifies and irritates Jack in equal measure: he does not believe in ghosts and is annoyed to be proved wrong.

The second half of this chapter provides us with more insights into the character of Jack's father, and into his parents' relationship. When Jack's mother was young, she went out with a young man called Ernie

Moore. Jack's father had also taken a fancy to her, however, and he approached her parents to ask for her hand in marriage. They agreed and, as this was an era in which girls like her obeyed their parents, in 1905 she married Jack's father, when she was seventeen and he was twenty-one.

Before Jack was born, his father served as a soldier during the War of Independence, although Jack says that this required nothing more than two years' marching around a field at weekends. The war, Jack claims, meant little to the men in Dalkey and did not usually affect their daily lives. The only exception to this was when Jack's uncle Johnny walked into a pub after a drilling exercise, still carrying his rifle, and found the place full of policemen. He was arrested but subsequently freed by his comrades before he could be tried and possibly shot. However, the incident threw suspicion on Jack's father's family. One night they were woken by the Black and Tans, who suspected them of hiding weapons in their house. Before the Tans could do much harm they were interrupted by a polite army officer, who apologised for the intrusion and took his men away. This was just as well, as there were two rifles hidden under Jack's parents' mattress.

Young Jack sees that his parents' marriage is a good one, although it has its moments of tension. One of these occurs when Jack's mother bumps into the woman who married her old boyfriend, Ernie Moore. The women have tea and cake together in a hotel, and Jack's mother is invited to tea in the Moores' house. On hearing this, Jack's father loses his temper and threatens his wife that if she accepts the invitation he will not be accountable for his actions. He is so furious that he is about to smash the milk jug to give vent to his feelings, but changes his mind and smashes his pipe instead. (Jack keeps the pieces and still has them at the time of writing the book.) Jack's mother responds hotly that Jack's father is only jealous because he knows that she was forced by her parents to marry him, when she preferred Ernie. Jack flees, horrified by this bitter talk. Only later, when he sees his mother's mixture of sadness that she can't accept the invitation to tea, and pride at her husband's jealousy, does Jack realise that adult relationships may not be as clear-cut as they first appear.

KEY QUESTIONS

- Why do you think Jack's father is pleased with the strange lump of tangled and burnt spectacles?

- What does this chapter tell us about the lives of members of the working class and the upper class?

- Jack's mother does not share her husband's affection for the Jacobs. Do you think this is simply a question of her wanting more money, or do you think that it shows a difference between her personality and Jack's father's personality?

- What mixed emotions do you think Jack might have felt on witnessing the fight between his parents?

- Why do you think Jack keeps the pieces of the pipe? Does this remind you of his father's keeping and valuing the burnt spectacles?

WRITING TASK

- Here are four descriptions of Jack's father: passionate; loyal; sentimental; loving. Choose the two that you most agree with and support your choice with reference to the novel.

Chapter 4

Jack recalls a typical evening spent with his father on a walk around their locality. They are accompanied by their dog. Jack's mother had appeared home one day with the scruffy creature and had told Jack and his father that the animal's name was also Jack, like the baby boy she had brought home equally unexpectedly some seven years before.

This chapter is significant because it shows the love Jack has for both his home place and his father. He names each place they passed on their walk together, which shows a nostalgic and appreciative remembrance of the area in which the author grew up.

As father and son walk, they chat about everything from the history of the area to ghost stories. That reminds Jack of something frightening and untrue that his aunt Chris told him: that his real mother spies on him at night and wants him back. Jack's parents had made up a story about his mother living on Lambay Island out in Dublin Bay and being unable to leave because she had to mind the seagulls there, but Chris told young Jack that his parents were lying to him. She terrified her young nephew with her tale of a tall, white-faced woman with a black coat looking through the window at him each night. Jack's father is angry, but consoles the boy with another invented story about his real mother, this time placing her on the Kish lightship, seven miles out to sea. Jack is somewhat relieved but still worried that the woman might have escaped from the lightship and be waiting for him when he gets home. He shares this fear with his father, who tells him not to worry as

he will kick Jack's real mother up the backside if she should be there. He threatens to do the same to Jack's aunt Chris and he is clearly very annoyed that she should have scared the boy with such a dreadful story. Jack is thrilled with his father's proposed solution, and reflects on how lucky he is to have the best father in Dalkey. To young Jack, Dalkey is his world, so this is a great compliment to his father.

The pair walk home, Jack holding his father's rough, work-worn hand and telling him that he loves him.

- **How well do you think Jack's father handles his son's fears about his birth mother?**

- **Does the way in which the story of Jack's adoption is dealt with by his family tell us anything about differences between attitudes in the thirties and those of today?**

KEY QUESTIONS

- **Imagine that Jack's father confronted Aunt Chris about the frightening story she told young Jack about his mother. Write the text of the speech he would be likely to make, explaining why he was so angry and what he would prefer the child to be told.**

WRITING TASK

Chapter 5

Jack the dog hates the clergy. Worse still, he only attacks Catholic clergy, which leads an unpleasant neighbour to hint that this hatred of priests and nuns is something the animal must have picked up from his owners.

One day the dog attacks a nun, who makes a complaint to the police. Unfortunately, the local guard (the 'Cat' McDonald) is a mean-spirited man who enjoys intimidating people. He threatens the Doyles with legal action. Jack's mother is appalled. She is terrified of the law and this situation sends her into a panic. When the guard offers them a way out by suggesting that they bring the dog to the police station to be shot, it is obvious that Jack's mother will leap at this chance to avoid court. The dog's fate seems to be sealed.

The next day, Jack is sent to the shop, but comes home just in time to see his father leading the dog towards the harbour. He realises immediately that his father's plan is to drown the dog, believing it to be both a humane way to dispose of the animal and a better option than giving the guard the satisfaction of shooting it. Jack runs after his father but only reaches the pier in time to see the dog – a concrete block attached to his collar – being thrown into the stormy sea. Amazingly, the dog swims to the surface of the water and, before his father can stop him, Jack runs down the steps towards the water. It is October and there is a gale blowing. The sea is very rough and the young boy is swept away by a wave. His father manages to pull both his son and the dog out of the water and the three head home together, soaked to the skin. The dog seems to regard the whole thing as a great adventure.

When they arrive back at the cottage they are astonished when Jack's mother rather hypocritically hugs the dog, tears streaming down her face. No prosecution results from the attack on the nun and Jack believes this may be because the 'Cat' McDonald is as disliked by his sergeant as he is by the local people.

The second half of this chapter is concerned with Jack's neighbourhood. His family live in one of five two-room cottages at the back gates of a large house belonging to the Pearsons, a wealthy Quaker family. Although the Pearsons do not own the terrace of five cottages, they act as if they do, and send their son to the Doyles' house every Christmas morning with a tin of sweets for young Jack. One year Jack decides to return the favour by presenting the Pearsons with a bag of broken chocolate pieces for their son, and although the gift is kindly received by the Pearsons, Jack's parents are horrified. They believe that Jack has embarrassed his family and has shown that he does not know his proper place in society.

> They believe that Jack has embarrassed his family and has shown that he does not know his proper place in society

There are a number of children living close by, so Jack is not short of playmates. One of the diversions the children enjoy is taunting Mr Redmond, a pro-British neighbour who is driven to shout threats at the youngsters when they chant republican rhymes outside his house. Although he roars and blusters, Mr Redmond would never dare lay a finger on the local children because he knows that their parents agree with these anti-British sentiments.

In his early years, Jack and the other neighbourhood boys and girls play on the lane close to his house. Their games are generally domestic in nature and organised by a tyrannical little girl called Teasie Costello. In time, the boys escape Teasie's rule and move on to Sorrento Park near the sea. The cinema is another attraction for the Dalkey youngsters and they derive much enjoyment from acting out the scenarios they have seen on the screen. Jack prefers to play the role of the bully rather than that of the hero as he feels there is more scope for the bully to fight and die in a dramatic fashion.

When the boys are older, they move their activities to an area known as the Fields. There they play cards and try out what they consider to be more adult behaviour, such as cursing and drinking. They usually have little more than a small bottle of flat stout to share, but they think that having even this makes them more manly.

The most exciting thing that happens during their time spent in the Fields is the appearance of a red deer during the war years. Jack joins a hundred or so locals who, with no clear idea of what they will do if they spot the deer, go hunting through the Fields. Jack is not very fit or active and soon lags behind the main group. As he stops to rest for a moment, he happens to see the deer peering at him from the middle of a hedge. They stare at each other for a few moments, then the deer jumps over the hedge and dashes off.

The author thinks back nostalgically to these early days as he reflects on how this whole neighbourhood has changed utterly in the years since he lived there. Now there are houses and a sports stadium where once there were green fields. Shortly before writing this book the author was asked to open a fashion show in the sports stadium and he was struck by the wealth of the people he hadn't seen since they, like him, were poor urchins in Dalkey. He wonders how his mother would have reacted had she seen the skimpy beachwear and nightdresses at the fashion show, and he imagines he can see her peering out of the kitchen window at the show in the stadium and asking his father what the world is coming to.

KEY
QUESTIONS

- Do you think that Jack's mother sees the law and those in authority as being there to help her or to oppress her?

- Do you think Jack's father was being cruel by trying to drown the dog?

- Jack's mother is delighted by the reappearance of the dog Jack after the failed drowning attempt. If that is the case, why do you think she insisted that the dog be destroyed in the first place?

- What does this chapter tell us about class distinction in Dublin in the thirties?

- List the similarities and differences you see between Jack's experience of growing up in his neighbourhood and those of a boy growing up in twenty-first-century Ireland. You may wish to consider some of the following: financial status, attitudes towards religion and authority, anti-British sentiment, class distinction, sense of community, friendship, leisure activities, etc.

- Write the report you think the local guard, 'Cat' McDonald, would have written about the complaint he received regarding Jack the dog and the visit he made to the Keyes' household.

WRITING TASK

Chapter 6

Sundays in Jack's household follow a regular pattern. Jack's mother goes to the Women's Mass at nine in the morning and Jack and his father go to 10.30 Mass. Jack's father fidgets and fusses while Jack eats his breakfast of white pudding and bread. Although they have plenty of time, Jack's father lives in fear of being late for anything, let alone Mass. When he can wait no longer, Jack's father flings open the door and leaves the house, young Jack hastily following.

The first person they meet on their way is Tish Meredith. Jack is too young to understand why this woman should spend her evenings standing on the side of the road, trying to attract the attention of passing men. His father does not enlighten him that Tish is a prostitute, and merely remarks that Tish is a 'harmless poor creature'. On Sundays, Tish seems shy and unsure of herself, as if she is not good enough for such a holy day.

As they walk on down the road, Jack sees another neighbour, Mrs Threadgold. He feels embarrassed when he spots her because he remembers an occasion some years before when he had been brought to her door by a neighbouring lad, Johnny Quinn. Jack had no idea why they were knocking on Mrs Threadgold's door and he did not hear what Johnny said to her. It was only when she handed them both a slice of bread and jam that he realised Johnny was begging. Jack knows that if his mother heard that he had been begging, she would be appalled and very angry. He is angry too, and resents Mrs Threadgold's lack of surprise that he came begging to her door. Jack hates her for implying that he is no better than his poorer neighbour, Johnny.

Jack and his father arrive at the church and take their place close to the middle of the congregation. The front seats are taken by the 'Quality' and the deeply religious people, while the back of the church is filled with those who want to be out of the door the moment Mass ends. As Jack sits in the crowded church, he hears wheezing, coughing and spluttering behind him. He turns to see Joe Healy, a local alcoholic who is clearly drunk.

> The front seats are taken by the 'Quality' and the deeply religious people, while the back of the church is filled with those who want to be out of the door the moment Mass ends

Mass begins and the congregation has mixed feelings on seeing that the gentle Father Clarke will be officiating. This means that the sermon will be read by Father Creedon, a large man with a loud, booming voice, who is not as tolerant as Father Clarke and who demands the congregation's full attention. As he speaks, Jack's mind wanders, but Father Creedon has a trick up his sleeve; he lets his voice drop to almost a whisper, then bellows loudly and suddenly. This makes Jack jump, but it has an even more dramatic effect on the sleeping Joe Healy, who leaps to his feet, shouting, 'Jasus, where am I?' Father Creedon is appalled and, rather than sensibly letting Joe fall asleep again, he demands that he leave the church immediately. Joe is too drunk to do so and falls into the side aisle. People jump up to see what is happening and Father Clarke, whether in an effort to avert further disturbances or because he genuinely believes the sermon is over, stands up and begins to say the prayers that follow the sermon. Father Creedon is furious at this interruption but can do nothing about it. Joe Healy is carried outside by some men and left to sleep it off in the church garden.

Mass is not the only ordeal Jack has to endure on Sundays. He also has to buy the newspapers in Mammy Reilly's shop. Mammy Reilly is a tiny, grubby, witch-like old lady. She never throws away unsold newspapers and they fill the shop almost to bursting point. Eventually they take up all the available space, apart from a tiny area inside the door where Mammy Reilly stands to serve customers. Mammy Reilly lives in the rooms behind the shop, but because the doorway to her living area is now blocked by stacks of newspapers, she has to engage in a bizarre ritual every day. In the morning, she climbs up a ladder and over the pile of newspapers, sliding down them to reach her space in the shop. In the evenings, she leaves the shop by the front door, goes through the sweetshop next door and over the back wall to her own living area.

Jack dreads buying the papers from Mammy Reilly because she tries to intimidate customers into giving her extra money by claiming that she has found an old bill of theirs. Most customers give in 'for a quiet life', but Jack's father refuses, so Jack has to face Mammy Reilly while his father walks on the far side of the street.

The rest of Sunday is far more pleasant, filled as it is with lemonade, a comic to read and a trip to the cinema. The family greatly enjoys the

excitement of following the serialised adventures of dashing aviator Ace Drummond or the exploits of Chinese-American detective Charlie Chan. Drummond, the cinema doorman, is regularly teased by the tougher boys and given the nickname 'Ace' or 'Bulldog' after another fictional character, Bulldog Drummond. Jack's mother loves the cinema and is naively thrilled by all the predictable twists and turns of the plot. After tea, aunt Chris and her husband come over to play cards. When they leave, Jack sits up in his bed listening contentedly to the radio while his parents read the Sunday papers at the kitchen table.

- **Why do you think Tish Meredith considers herself unworthy for a holy day?**

- **This chapter is notable for the description of various local characters. Do you think they are well drawn? Re-read this chapter in the novel to help you write your answer.**

- **Read the section in the novel that deals with the incident in the church. Do you think it is humorous? Does the use of dialogue help bring the story to life?**

- **Overall, do you think that young Jack enjoys Sundays? You might refer to the text itself, particularly the last paragraph of Chapter 6, to help you form an opinion.**

WRITING TASK

- **Does the description of a typical Sunday in young Jack's life appeal to you? Give reasons for your answer.**

Chapter 7

The author opens this chapter by telling us that two important things happened when he was thirteen: he stopped going to confession; and he killed Mrs Kelly, who lived on his road.

Young Jack usually confesses his sins to the gentle Father Clarke: he was a chaplain in the army during World War I, and is inclined to look on his Dalkey congregation's sins as being nothing at all compared to the horrors he saw during his four years in the trenches. Father Clarke's easy-going manner and speedy confessions make him very popular and there is usually a queue waiting to see him.

One day, however, Jack finds to his dismay that Father Clarke has been promoted to his own parish and that Father Creedon will be hearing confessions in his place. Jack waits in dread for his turn and when he does finally get to speak to Father Creedon, he rushes to confess his sins. He is halted in his tracks by the priest's insistence that he says the Confiteor, a prayer that most priests allow penitents to say privately before they enter the confessional. Jack is nervous and makes a mess of the recitation. Father Creedon is appalled and throws Jack out of the confession box, ordering him to kneel in the church until the rest of the confessions are over, at which time he will be given a prayer book and will learn the Confiteor properly. Jack leaves the box in shame and, unable to bear the thought of facing Father Creedon again, he runs away and goes to another church to say confession.

That is not the end of the matter, of course. Father Creedon meets Jack's father later in the day and accosts him in the middle of the street. Jack's father is not a huge fan of the clergy since they excommunicated some of the fighters during the Civil War. That he should now be shamed by Father Creedon publicly asking him if his family ever prays together enrages Nick Keyes.

Jack is not so much upset as angered by this incident. He feels that Father Creedon has violated the sanctity of the confessional by repeating something he heard in confidence. Jack, who is heavily influenced by his weekly trips to the cinema, recalls how a priest in a recent film was 'ready to let an innocent man go to the electric chair sooner than repeat what he had heard in the confessional'. Father Creedon, in Jack's eyes, falls far short of this priestly ideal. Jack resolves to stop going to confession in protest at Father Creedon's revelation. He admits, however, that it suits him perfectly well to have a good reason to avoid doing something he dislikes.

This religious crisis of conscience is made even worse some months later when Jack comes to believe that he is responsible for the death of old Mrs Kelly down the road. Mrs Kelly regularly takes to her bed and announces that she is dying, but she invariably recovers at the last minute. Jack's mother is summoned to help whenever Mrs Kelly gets one of her turns.

On this particular night, Jack is out visiting a friend while his mother attends to Mrs Kelly. Heading home after his evening out, Jack sees a light on in Mrs Kelly's house, so he knows that his mother is still there.

He decides to let her know that he is safely on his way home, so he raps sharply on the window to get her attention. Suddenly he hears a strange voice from inside, shouting out in terror, 'The Dead Man's Knock! The Dead Man's Knock!' Appalled by the reaction to his innocent tapping, Jack flees.

It is one o'clock in the morning before Jack's mother arrives home. Jack is sure that she will scold him for being awake at that hour, but she seems too preoccupied to do so and the reason soon becomes clear. Mrs Kelly died that night and Jack's mother believes that her death was inevitable because they had heard the 'Dead Man's Knock'.

Jack's guilt eventually fades, but the whole incident convinces him that he is 'one of nature's outcasts'. For some reason that is never clear, even to himself, Jack decides that (having committed the most dreadful sin there is) he might as well break the other nine commandments and 'have done with it'. He manages to break several quite easily, but finds himself in trouble when it comes to committing the last sin on his list. The problem is that he is not sure what adultery is. His first attempt to find out, by asking Father Creedon on one of his visits to the school, is disastrous. Both Father Creedon and Jack's teacher are sure that the boy is being cheeky and he is punished for his insolence. In desperation, Jack asks his father what adultery is. His father seems puzzled at first, but recovers himself and demonstrates what he believes adultery to be by pouring water into a cup containing some milk. It is only years later that Jack realises his father had confused adultery and dilution.

> Jack decides that (having committed the most dreadful sin there is) he might as well break the other nine commandments and 'have done with it'

KEY QUESTIONS

- We met Father Creedon in the previous chapter as well as this one. What sort of person do you think he is?

- What does this chapter tell us about the author's attitude towards religion? Do you, for example, think that Father Creedon is genuinely interested in people's spiritual well-being or is he more interested in having an obedient and respectful congregation?

- If Jack's father is not keen on the clergy since they excommunicated some fighters during the Civil War, why do you think he continues to go to Mass and does not stand up for himself when Father Creedon accosts him in the street?

- In the book, Jack says, 'The last person I would normally ask for information or advice was my father.' Why do you think this is?

- Write *three* diary entries that you think Jack might have written after the events in this chapter. You may wish to consider his 'killing' Mrs Kelly, his attempts to break the commandments, and his feelings after his conversation with his father at the end of the chapter.

WRITING
TASK

Chapter 8

Shortly before his fourteenth birthday, Jack starts at Presentation College. He has won a scholarship, much to his mother's delight. She pretends to ask the neighbours' advice about which school she should send Jack to, but all she really wants is a chance to tell them about the scholarship. She is so excited that she even tells her brother Sonny, forgetting that they had been fighting since their sister Mary came to live with Jack's family after Jack's grandmother's death. Sonny likes to pretend that his beloved Mary was stolen from him, even though he is actually pleased to see the back of her. Sonny implies that Jack somehow got the scholarship by cunning rather than intelligence, and the brother's and sister's fight begins anew.

Jack's mother takes offence easily, like all her family. Jack remembers a time when his mother went to visit her sister Chris in hospital and Chris did not introduce her to another visitor as her sister. Jack's mother knew that Chris was ashamed of her sister's poor clothes and her obvious working-class background. But that fight was some time ago and the rift has healed by the time Jack gets the scholarship. Chris recommends that Jack attend Presentation College as she feels that a nicer class of boy goes there than to the Christian Brothers school. Jack is delighted at this suggestion because he wants to go to

© AMALGAMATED PRESS

Presentation College and imagines that he can reinvent himself there and be whoever he wants to be. He is an avid reader of *The Magnet* (a boys' paper) and its stories about Greyfriars, a fictional English public school. To him, Presentation College seems a similar place to Greyfriars and a million miles from the schools and classmates he is used to. Greyfriars pupils are either Bullies (villains) or Chaps (heroes) and Jack has high hopes of being one of the Chaps.

Jack's mother brings him to meet the Superior of the Presentation College, Brother Berchmans Morley. He is an unfriendly looking man with a long nose – hence his nickname, 'Schnozzle'. Jack waits outside the office while his mother and Brother Berchmans chat. Jack is lost in daydreams of the wonderful time he will have in this place and how different it will be from the schools he is used to. His mother reappears a few minutes later and they head home. To Jack's dismay, he discovers that she has told Brother Berchmans all about Jack's adoption, which he would rather have kept secret; but he consoles himself with the thought that, like the masters at his beloved Greyfriars, Brother Berchmans is bound to be too honourable to share this information.

Jack's schooling to date has been at the Loreto Convent and Harold Boys' School. His principal memory of his time in Loreto is being unfairly accused of telling tales out of school. He had been punished by a nun one day for dirtying his copybook, although it had been an accident. A neighbouring girl had told his parents about the incident and Jack's father had gone to the school and complained about this unfair treatment. The nun in question had assumed Jack had told tales and he didn't even try to correct her because 'once they had it in their minds that you were the Bully, it was a waste of time trying to act the Chap.'

Neither was his time in Harold Boys' the stuff of *The Magnet*. Even when he tried to do the right thing, it never quite worked out. While in the class of the fearsome headmaster, Tabac (the Irish word for tobacco), Jack and the other boys were each given charge of a flower-bed in the schoolyard. Eager to find a plant that would grow quickly and need little care, Jack asked his father for help. His father gave him a packet of seeds along with an instruction to use them very sparingly. Jack ignored the advice and scattered the entire contents of the packet. The flowers emerged a few days later and Jack saw, to his horror, that they had taken over not only his bed but all the others as well. The flower-bed experiment was deemed a failure. Later, Jack questioned his father and discovered that the flowers he planted were called 'Mother o' Millions'.

Jack hopes that he will make a fresh start at Presentation College and is dismayed to find that his father will be accompanying him on his first day. He does not want his new classmates to see his father in his shabby working clothes. When they reach the school, Jack says goodbye to his father and runs off quickly. He reaches the schoolyard and stands close to a group of boys with whom he hopes to make friends. This plan is ruined, however, by his father peering in at the gate and waving at him. One of the other boys begins to mock Jack's father's obvious poverty and asks Jack if the 'old gentleman' belongs to him. Cornered and ashamed, Jack punches the other boy on the nose. The bell rings for the start of the school day and Jack feels like crying as he realises that he is like the worst sort of bully in *The Magnet* and a million miles away from the fine fellow he had hoped to be.

One of the other boys begins to mock Jack's father's obvious poverty and asks Jack if the 'old gentleman' belongs to him

Things do not improve as the day wears on. Brother Berchmans comes into Jack's class and hands out raffle tickets for the boys to sell. When he comes to Jack, he decides not to give him any tickets, fearing that he might be leading Jack 'into temptation'. It takes Jack a moment to realise that Brother Berchmans fears that Jack will steal any money he raises. This sets the seal on Jack's acceptance of the fact that his dream of a Greyfriars-type education is over.

KEY
QUESTIONS

- Why do you think Jack's mother tells Brother Berchmans that Jack was adopted?

- Why do you think Jack reacts so violently to the boy who comments on his father's appearance?

- Do you think that Jack ever had a chance of reinventing himself in Presentation College?

- What are the main differences between Irish education in the thirties and forties and Irish education in the twenty-first century?

**WRITING
TASK**

- Jack is delighted when he receives his scholarship to Presentation College and imagines that school life will be just like it is in his favourite stories. However, the dream quickly turns sour. What are the reasons for this, do you think?

Chapter 9

The author's years in Presentation College are not the happy ones of his imagining. He does not fit in and becomes the victim of a gang of bullies who are determined to expose and mock his working-class background. One lad even follows him home regularly in order to see Jack's small house but Jack knows what he is up to and leads him on a merry dance all around Dalkey rather than going home.

Eventually, Jack turns to cruel, witty insults as a way of gaining some favour with the other boys. He achieves some measure of success with this as he has an excellent way with words, but he does not make any lasting friends in the school. Neither has he any great affection for the staff.

The Superior of the college is a snobbish, unhappy, resentful man who drinks to excess. His unhappiness may stem in part from the fact that he is rumoured to have been forced into the religious life. He hates the boys and takes pleasure in administering beatings when the pupils incur his displeasure. During Jack's final year at the school, the Superior is transferred to a religious house whose aim is to deal with 'misfits, backsliders and rebels' and he eventually leaves religious life completely.

Physical punishment is a regular part of school life and Jack recalls one particular incident in which a boy named Dinkie Meldrum is badly beaten for questioning the power of prayer. Dinkie has a name as a rebel, and a teacher, the normally easy-going Brother Alfie, completely loses his temper at what he considers Dinkie's 'aesthetic communism'. He thrashes Dinkie with the cane until blood is drawn and the cane breaks. Far from being disciplined for this savage beating, Brother Alfie is praised by the other teachers for defending the faith. Dinkie Meldrum, who had largely been ignored by the staff up to this point, now becomes the target for all the teachers' worst punishments. After a few weeks of this, Dinkie has had enough. When Brother Alfie reaches for the cane again one day, the boy darts out of the door, locking it behind him. He strolls out of the school, singing a dirty song, and is never seen again.

Corporal punishment is the accepted means of disciplining pupils, and even the boys themselves expect it. They regard one of their lay teachers as weak because he never hits his students. The boys torment him and feel a 'sense of power' in denying him respect. One night the teacher falls to his death from the upstairs window of his house and the author suspects that he may have taken his own life, partly driven to it by the daily humiliation and mockery doled out by the pupils in his charge.

Jack's favourite teacher among the Presentation Brothers is Seraphim. He is a kindly man in his sixties who suffers from a condition which causes his head to nod perpetually. He teaches the boys Irish and English. His real love is English, particularly Shakespeare. Prince Hal (Henry V of England and a major character in several of Shakespeare's history plays) is his hero and Seraphim regularly extols his virtues. Seraphim's mortal enemy is another teacher, Brother Athanasius, and matters between them come to a head when Athanasius acts as a substitute for Seraphim, who is ill with flu. Nearing recovery, Seraphim returns to class one day to observe Athanasius teaching and is horrified to hear his rival call Prince Hal a 'consummate hypocrite' and 'a typical two-faced Englishman'. Unable to contain himself, Seraphim staggers to his feet and calls Athanasius an 'ignorant ruffian'. Athanasius is initially reluctant to respond to Seraphim's insults because he does not want the boys to see disunity among the staff, but he is stung into calling Seraphim 'a disgrace to the cloth' and, much to the boys' delight, the pair are soon trading insults and threats. Seraphim, fuelled with indignation at the criticism of his beloved Hal, wins the day and Athanasius flees the room, appalled. Content with his victory, Seraphim takes up the lesson where Athanasius had left off.

Jack's time at Presentation College is not a productive one. He loses interest in school, partly because he feels he does not belong there,

> Jack's time at Presentation College is not a productive one. He loses interest in school, partly because he feels he does not belong there

and as a result he has to repeat fourth year twice until his scholarship runs out. His mother pretends to her neighbours and friends that Jack is being kept in fourth year because he is so good, while the other pupils are 'shifted' out of the class. She knows that this is not the truth and warns Jack to say nothing of his progress to his aunt Chris and her husband John, who would not be so easily fooled.

Seven years after leaving school, the author (now beginning to make a name as a writer and an actor) is invited back to direct Christmas plays. Brother Berchmans and Brother Seraphim are long gone, and the author is surprised to see that the Brothers, 'yesterday's tyrants', are now revealed as ordinary men. This impression is consolidated when the author has a drink and a chat with the new Superior, a Kerryman who is 'bubbling with good humour'. The Superior reveals that he never intended to join the religious order but drifted into it because the Presentation Brothers paid for his secondary school and university education.

KEY QUESTIONS
- **Why do you think Jack disliked his time in Presentation College?**

- Why do you think Jack's mother tries to keep his academic failure a secret from Chris and John Bennett?

- From your reading of this chapter, what impression do you form of religious-led education in Ireland at the time the novel was written?

- Imagine young Jack has been invited to your school to give a talk about his experiences in Presentation College. Write the text of the talk you think he would give.

WRITING TASK

Chapter 10

Jack's father now works for the new owners of Enderley. They are a Catholic family and Jack's father finds them difficult employers. He resents working for people who are so like himself. He has a small pension from the years he spent working for the Jacobs, and while he is happy to receive this, Jack's mother awaits the monthly cheque with a mixture of impatience and resentment. She has never forgiven the Jacob family for the small lump sum and worthless gift given to Jack's father on his retirement. On the rare occasions when the Jacobs' daughter, Mrs Pim, comes to visit, Jack's father greets her with pleasure and enjoys talking about the old days, while Jack's mother remains tight-lipped and silent.

Jack has to write a regular 'thank you' letter to Mrs Pim for the money received. He is called back to do this one sunny Sunday, when he has arranged to meet his friend Oliver, so he is in a temper as he sits down to write the letter. His mother instructs him to inform Mrs Pim that he has left school but is hoping to find work. The eighteen-year-old Jack has had no work since leaving school, apart from a brief appearance as an extra in a film version of *Henry V*. In the letter he compares himself to Mr Micawber, a feckless character from Charles Dickens' *David Copperfield* who is always 'waiting for something to turn up'. His mother does not understand the reference and orders him to rewrite the letter. He is scornful of her ignorance and corrects her grammar when she reprimands him, telling him to 'do it proper'. At this, his mother loses her temper and cruelly says that the Pims and his former classmates in Presentation College must have laughed at Jack's attempts to pretend that he is as good as them. She goes even further, pointing out that at least she and Jack's father are not illegitimate, unlike him. It is only years later that the author realises that these hurtful words were merely proof that 'love turned upside-down is love for all that'. As an eighteen-year-old, however, he is filled with hatred and anger, and makes to leave the room. His mother blocks his way and, despite himself, he feels a smile rising at her turn of speed. He refuses to rewrite the letter, but his mother enlists his father's aid and, anxious to have a peaceful Sunday, his father orders him to write the letter again. Jack does so, but in such a way that it is, unbeknownst to his parents, more disrespectful than before.

Having escaped the unpleasant chore of letter writing, Jack heads off to his friend Oliver's house. Oliver's mother won £500 in a crossword competition some years before and it turned her head completely. She became unpredictable; friendly one minute and aggressive the next. When Oliver's family lived in their last home they had heard noises that suggested the house was haunted, and people were quick to say that this had something to do with Oliver's mother's sudden windfall. There were hints of a pact with the devil. When the family moved to another house, however, the ghostly noises in the old house continued, which seemed to prove that they had nothing to do with Oliver's mother. The new tenants asked Father Creedon to perform an exorcism, which he did with his usual drama. He marched into the house, spraying holy water liberally before him, and vanished from sight. There was silence for a time, until a small boy went into the house and reappeared suddenly, shouting: 'It's coming out.' The waiting crowd stampeded and Father Creedon, on emerging from the house, was disappointed to see that nobody remained to see how he had got on.

Oliver now lives a mile or so away from Jack's house, and is still getting ready to go out when Jack arrives. Oliver is fussy about his appearance and will not leave the house until every last detail of his outfit is perfect. He has had no formal education – his mother took him out of national school and then, being a 'contrary sort', did not get around to enrolling him in secondary school – but Oliver is not concerned. He believes in self-education and pursues it with mixed results. For example, while he knows a little philosophy, he mispronounces the name of the philosopher Descartes, calling him 'Des Carty'.

Oliver is not like the other boys in Jack's gang, and they are not sure what to make of him. Most of the boys are apprenticed to various tradesmen and therefore have their futures mapped out, but Oliver is something of a mystery. Nobody knows what he will become. One of the things Jack finds difficult about Oliver is the other boy's independence. If anybody picks a fight with him, he merely drifts away, unperturbed. He does not seem to need anyone.

Despite all this, or perhaps because of it, Oliver is very attractive to women. They fawn over him and seem willing to do anything he wants. Oliver is a great believer in self-control and gives nothing away when the other lads ask him how far he has got with a particular girl. Oliver likes his girlfriends until the point where they feel that they have ownership over him. If that happens, he quietly but firmly leaves them.

KEY QUESTIONS

- Read the first page of this chapter in the novel and then explain why you think Jack's father dislikes working for people like himself.

- Years after the incident in which his mother used the fact of his illegitimacy to wound him, the author realises that these hurtful words were merely proof that 'love turned upside-down is love for all that'. Do you agree with him?

- Why do you think Jack's mother speaks so hurtfully to her son?

- Why do Jack's parents not realise that his second version of the letter is less respectful than the first, even though they check it?

- What is your impression of Jack's friend Oliver?

**WRITING
TASK**

• **Write the first letter that you think Jack might have written
to the Jacobs, before his mother insisted that he rewrite it.**

Chapter 11

Oliver is one of the few people from Jack's childhood who never
changes. Years later, he is still living in a council house and seems
unable to hold down a job for long. Yet he is very happy, and married
with a family. The author says that although Oliver 'never talks about
the past', he never left it.

The outbreak of war in 1939 does not affect Jack or his family in any
major way, except for the privations of rationing. Food and fuel are
scarce during 'The Emergency'.

Apart from one bombing raid, the war does not really touch Dublin.
Jack is keen to play his part in defending his country, so he joins
various organisations, including the Emergency Communication
Corps and the Local Defence Force. He is not notably successful in
these organisations and during one exercise with the Local Defence
Force he even leads his unit directly into the arms of the 'enemy'.
Realising that he will be reprimanded for this, Jack simply goes home
and never returns to his unit. Despite this failure, Jack decides to join
the Local Security Force as an auxiliary policeman. One night he is sent
out on patrol with a man named Devaney. Devaney is gay, and he
believes that the more men he approaches sexually, the greater his
chance of success. This sexual lottery fails when he makes a move on
Jack. Jack, horrified and bewildered by the advance, headbutts
Devaney and gives him a bloody nose. The pair return to headquarters
where the duty sergeant, obviously aware of Devaney's attraction to
young men, admonishes him severely and, in frustration, strikes him
with a heavy book. Devaney bursts into tears and the sergeant sends
Jack home while at the same time warning him not to say anything
about Devaney, 'dirty elders and all as he is'.

Jack's adolescence is marked by his desire to leave the nest, yet at

Recruitment poster for Ireland's Local Defence Force published during World War II

the same time he mourns the loss of the happy childhood days spent on long walks with his father. His father makes Jack's transition from child to adult easy by affecting not to notice that his son is growing up, but his mother has such a strong influence over him that he even pretends to her that he does not drink so that she can't make him feel guilty about it.

The teenage Jack's life is heavily influenced by his almost daily trips to the cinema. It doesn't matter how dreadful or predictable the films are, Jack and his friends sit through them all and revel in the chance to briefly escape their own lives and lose themselves in the onscreen adventures and romances.

Jack's best friends are Dan, Liam and Joe. Dan and Liam are going out with girls they later marry, while Joe and Jack date a series of girls. Although Joe boasts about his sexual exploits, when Jack reveals that he actually touched his date's breasts he is appalled. He covers up his initial shock by teasing Jack in front of the other lads, but Jack now knows that, for all his talk, Joe is as inexperienced as he is.

Jack and his friends parade along the seafront for several years in the sure knowledge that they will move on to better things in the future. They look with pity on Tommy Martin, a middle-aged veteran of the Easter Rising of 1916 who spends his days trying to befriend the youngsters who hang around the area. Tommy was shot in the ankle during that conflict and seemed set to earn a pension for life until he lost his entire leg in a motorcycle accident almost twenty years later. Because the injured ankle was amputated, Tommy lost his pension along with it. Some feel that Tommy befriends young lads because he is lonely, but others are convinced that he is a degenerate. Whatever the reason, Jack's friends are kind to the older man and ignore his irritating ways. Jack doesn't share his friends' diplomacy and uses his quick wits to make a fool of the rather pathetic older man.

KEY QUESTIONS

- This chapter tells us a little about attitudes towards sexuality in Ireland in the forties. What differences do you see between the attitudes then and the attitudes in twenty-first-century Ireland?

- Why do you think the cinema was such an important part of Jack's life?

WRITING TASK

- 'Jack's relationships with his parents and his friends are not always easy.' Do you agree or disagree with this statement? Support your answer by referring to the novel.

Chapter 12

It has been six months since Jack left school and his family has decided that a job in the civil service would be ideal for him. Jack's parents arrange for him to meet Mr Drumm, a local man who works in the Land Commission, in the hope that he will give Jack a good reference. Although Mr Drumm knows Jack's father a little, he does not know Jack at all and seems reluctant to do much to help him join the civil service, a career move that he says he would not recommend to anyone. Jack's father says cheerfully that such a job will do Jack for now and that once the war is over there will be plenty of work. Mr Drumm disagrees, but Jack's father is on a roll and assures Mr Drumm that once the Germans defeat the English they will hand out great jobs to the Irish. He praises Hitler and scorns Winston Churchill. Jack's father is not really pro-Nazi, but rather he hates the English and supports anyone who opposes them.

Mr Drumm is unimpressed by this pro-German talk and suggests that he and Jack go for a walk together so that he can get to know the young man for whom he is supposed to write a reference. Jack leaves the room briefly to get the civil service forms, returning just in time to hear his mother telling the old story of his adoption. It seems that she will not allow Jack to shake off the ignominy of his earliest days, and he is angry and embarrassed to think that this tale will now follow him into his working life.

Mr Drumm takes Jack to a pub and, during their conversation, asks him bluntly what his real name is. Jack is surprised at the question and stunned when Mr Drumm points out that, as Jack is illegitimate, his surname must be different from that of his adoptive parents. Mr Drumm is unrepentant when he sees that his question has nearly reduced Jack to tears, telling Jack that he has no real reason to feel sorry for himself and that it is up to him to make something of his life. Mr Drumm has little respect for most of his fellow men. He claims that working-class men are ignorant and 'not a damn bit of good'.

> Mr Drumm is unrepentant when he sees that his question has nearly reduced Jack to tears

Jack's father escapes the worst of Mr Drumm's censure because he at least does an honest day's work and is an amusing character. Mr Drumm speaks equally unflatteringly about his colleagues in the civil service, describing those who speak Irish as 'clodhoppers and fanatics' who 'smell of manure and have to be etherised before they'll put a collar and tie on'.

Jack is bewildered by Mr Drumm's sharp tongue and his bitter criticisms of others. He feels uneasy and, worried that his own answers to Mr Drumm's questions are being carefully noted and judged, makes his excuses and leaves as soon as possible. Mr Drumm is displeased with Jack's obvious desire to get away and dismisses him curtly.

A month later, much to his parents' delight, Jack is called for an interview in the civil service. His father uncomplainingly takes on extra work every evening for two weeks in order to earn money to buy a suit for Jack, despite Jack's guilty protestations that he does not need a suit and would rather his father spent the money on himself.

The interview is a success and Jack is offered a job in the Land Commission. He wonders if he will be working with his uncle John but is instead put in Mr Drumm's section.

The work is boring and Jack hates it. He can't believe he was so foolish as to allow his mother and his aunt Chris to persuade him to take the position just because it is secure and pays reasonably well. Jack reflects bitterly that it is his own fault for giving in to them 'because Yes was always easier to say than No'. He wonders how he will survive in such a tedious job and he dreams of escape. As the weeks pass, he learns a little about his colleagues. There are a number of interesting characters, but even they are not enough to make Jack enjoy his job. He longs to 'be free of that place', and when he has been there for six months he gets a glimpse of a possible alternative future. A colleague has been to see Seán O'Casey's *The Plough and the Stars* and

recommends that Jack go and see it too. Jack has never been to the theatre before and his night at the Abbey changes his life for ever. He is enchanted by the brilliance of the play and the acting. Now he burns with desire to be part of this world and he knows that he has found 'the door he would escape through'.

KEY QUESTIONS

- What is your impression of Mr Drumm?

- Do you think that Jack's father has really thought out his political beliefs?

- Why do you think Jack allows himself to be sent into a job in the civil service if it is not something he particularly wants?

- Why do you think Jack dislikes the civil service so much?

- Do you think that Jack has taken much control of his life to date?

- What do you think Jack means when he says that the theatre has shown him 'the door he would escape through'?

WRITING TASK

- Write the diary entry you think Jack might have written after his trip to the theatre.

Chapter 13

Jack's father may be troubled by arthritis and increasing deafness as he ages, but he does not let that stop him carrying on as he always has done. When he is knocked down by a motor scooter and hospitalised, his only concern is that, because his hand is injured, he cannot cut up the tobacco for his pipe.

In 1948, trams are replaced by buses and the author and his father join a crowd of locals to watch as the tram that has served their neighbourhood for decades takes its last journey through the area. The end of the tram service signals the end of an era. According to the author, the new era is one of people who have money but no class. He describes them as 'the jumped up and the dragged up'. These newly rich people view Jack's father with suspicion because he is a reminder of their own poor backgrounds. To the Jacobs, he had been 'a breed apart, a separate species: he was a servant to be looked after and left alone'. Jack's father respects the 'quality' of the past but has no time for his new employers.

As his father's world changes, the author's world is changing too. He refuses to accept that his future lies in the civil service and he endures his fourteen years there because he is sure that he will eventually find a means of escape.

Mr Drumm is the author's superior for eleven years. Their relationship is changeable, to say the least. Mr Drumm takes offence at the slightest thing and his moods are impossible to predict. For some reason that Jack never discovers, he invokes Mr Drumm's displeasure and is thereafter viewed as an enemy rather than an

The number 8 DUTC tram that ran between Nelson's Pillar in O'Connell Street and Dalkey

ally. Mr Drumm has little respect for his superiors and this inevitably leads to his being 'promoted' to a position which requires him to sit in a room on his own, dealing with paperwork.

Eventually, the author's success as a playwright enables him to leave the civil service. On his last day, a colleague tells Jack that he should say goodbye to Mr Drumm. Reluctantly, Jack does so. He is surprised by Mr Drumm's emotional reaction to the news that his former protégé is leaving. Mr Drumm wishes Jack well and their former quarrel is not mentioned. Six years after leaving the civil service, Jack's mother dies and he sees Mr Drumm at her funeral. He visits his former boss's home and is warmly received. The author is sufficiently moved to send Mr Drumm tickets to his latest play and is resigned but unsurprised to receive a 'formal and detailed critique of the play' some weeks later. Gratitude and flattery, it seems, are not ideas to which Mr Drumm subscribes.

The author's father lives on for another two years after his wife's death, though he deteriorates to the extent that he has to move into sheltered accommodation. It is Mr Drumm who leads the campaign to have the author's father declared a 'public nuisance' and put into care. The author goes into considerable detail about the efforts he made at the time to get his father to move to London to live with him. He also refers to an expert opinion (from a doctor friend) advising that his father should remain in Dublin and move into sheltered accommodation. In the end, however, even this option proves unsuitable as the elderly man's mind begins to fail and he becomes increasingly difficult to deal with.

The author's father is moved to a psychiatric hospital and dies there. In the same year, Mr Drumm passes away.

Two years later, in 1970, the author moves back to Dublin for good. As he drives towards the city on his return, he remembers another journey home, many years before. His memory is of himself as a small boy, out collecting sticks for the fire and realising suddenly that it is growing dark and that he must run if he is to be home before night. The book ends with the author's sentimental recollection of his seven- or eight-year-old self hurrying back to the welcoming warmth of his family's small cottage, where his father and mother wait anxiously for his safe return.

- In what ways does this chapter mark the end of an era?

- In this chapter, do you think that the author is still trying to reassure himself and others that he made the right decision in relation to his elderly father's care?

- Does the ending of the book give you a final impression of the author's attitude towards his upbringing? How would you describe this attitude?

KEY QUESTIONS

- The author calls Mr Drumm 'an impossible man'. From your reading of Chapters 12 and 13, do you agree or disagree with this statement?

WRITING TASK

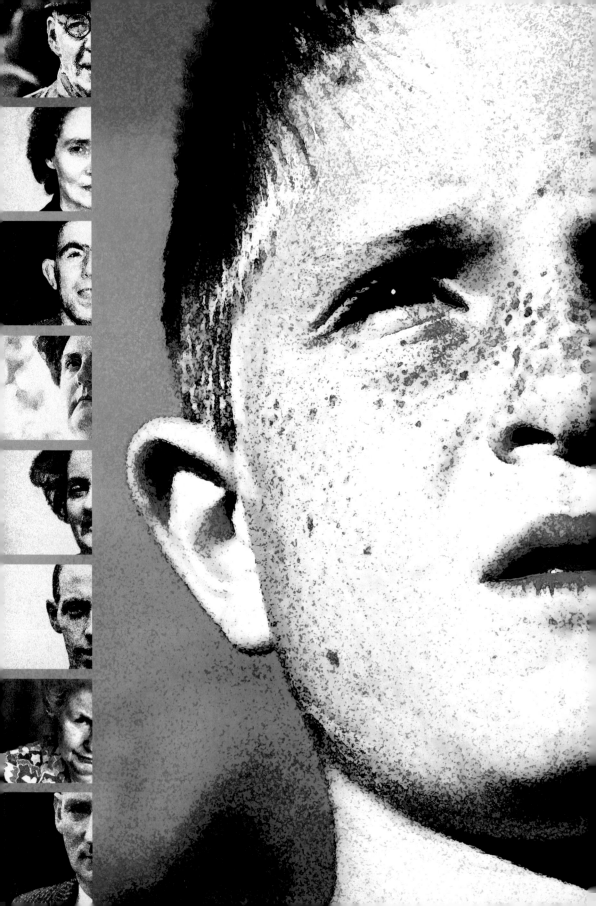

Character
analysis

2

Jack Keyes Byrne

The author

happy child
honest
self-deprecating
class-conscious
intelligent
well-read
cynical

Has a happy childhood

It is easy to make sweeping negative judgements about Jack's relationship with his parents, but it is important to look at those relationships in the context of the time. Ireland in the thirties and forties was a very different place from twenty-first-century Ireland, and parents and children did not necessarily interact in the same way that they do nowadays.

The author describes his childhood in Dalkey with a great deal of affection. The characters and the setting are richly recreated, and although there was little money, he does not seem to have felt that he lacked anything. His mother and father are not portrayed as perfect parents, but Jack loves them and is proud of them despite their failings. He recalls the many trips to the cinema with his mother, and the evening walks around Dalkey with his father. In Chapter 6, Jack describes a typical Sunday with his family full of simple pleasures such as going to the cinema, having lemonade with dinner, a new comic. The young boy finds it hard to imagine anything better than rushing home after Mass 'to open the bag of sweets that was Sunday'.

There are sad moments in Jack's childhood, of course, but they are outweighed by the positive memories. In the second chapter, Jack describes his mother ruining a family outing by becoming drunk and quarrelsome; she gets involved in an argument with a stranger as the family disembarks from the *Royal Iris*, a boat on which they had cruised around the harbour. Jack is embarrassed and distressed by his mother's behaviour, but when a passing woman tries to comfort him he is unimpressed. She gives him some money and he thinks of the sweets he will buy with it, the same sweets his mother always buys when they go to the cinema: even in his misery, the happy moments he has spent with his family give Jack some solace. His loyalty is to his parents and he is relieved when they suddenly appear and his father scoops him up in his arms 'the way a snowball would pick up a stone'. As they wait for the train to take them home, Jack wonders how long it will be before he is not ashamed to be seen in public after his mother's embarrassing behaviour. He imagines that he should be safe by Christmas and he recalls the wonderful times he and his mother have in town, visiting not one but two Santas and having lunch in Pim's. Although his imagination betrays him and he sees in his mind's eye people recognising them as 'the woman and the boy off the *Royal Iris*', it is still clear that he has a stock of happy memories to draw on and that unpleasant occasions are the exception rather than the norm.

'the way a snowball would pick up a stone'

Jack lives in a close community and has many friends. His journey from childhood through adolescence and on to young adulthood is 'measured by playgrounds'. He and his friends progress from spending their time playing at 'house' or 'shop' in the lane outside their houses to more boyish rough-and-tumble games in Sorrento Park, and finally to playing cards and drinking in The Fields. In each case, the playground is a little further away from home, but the security of growing up in the company of childhood friends remains the same.

Haunted by the story of his adoption

Jack's mother is fond of telling everyone the story of his adoption. She does so to gain sympathy and admiration for her selflessness in taking on a sickly and unwanted child. Jack loathes having the tale told and tries in vain to escape the stigma associated with his illegitimacy. However, each attempt to do so is met with failure. He hopes to reinvent himself when he starts secondary school, but his mother loses no time telling the principal 'how she had adopted him when his own didn't want him'. Even when he leaves school and starts work in the civil service, Jack cannot keep his adoption secret. To Jack's dismay, his mother tells Mr Drumm all about it when he visits the house.

While modern-day readers might find it surprising that Jack is so keen to keep the story of his birth under wraps, it must be remembered that illegitimacy was viewed as shameful in the Ireland of this period. Some people viewed a child born outside wedlock as less trustworthy or decent than a child born of married parents.

An honest and self-deprecating narrator

The author does little to present himself in a flattering light in this novel, mostly for comic effect. Even when he tries to save the family dog from drowning – which might be seen as admirable – Jack is quick to point out that he has no idea why he did something so out of character. It would have been more typical, he claims, for him to 'slouch off in solitary misery'.

Jack is not a particularly strong or fit youngster. He is tall, skinny and prone to fainting fits. He is not particularly attractive to women and when he and his friend Joe pick up a couple of nurses one evening, Jack is not surprised that he is left 'with the fatter and the plainer of the two'. He is sexually inexperienced and naively believes his friends when they talk of their exploits with girls. This backfires badly when Jack finally manages to touch his date's breasts and tells his friend Joe about it. Joe is horrified and it is only then that Jack realises that there had been no truth in the other lads' boasting but that it was simply a game they played. Far from being admired for his prowess with the opposite sex, Jack is once again cast in the role of The Bully, much to his disappointment.

> Jack is not a particularly strong or fit youngster. He is tall, skinny and prone to fainting fits

Class conscious and keen to reinvent himself

Jack resembles his mother more than his father when it comes to issues of class. She is aware of her position in society but enjoys any opportunity to mix with those of a higher social class. Jack takes this desire further and dreams of becoming one of the 'quality'. These ideas are partly fuelled by the English schoolboy comics he reads, such as *The Magnet*. He identifies with the heroes of the stories and looks forward to attending Presentation College where he imagines school life will be the same as it is in the stories he loves so much. He is deeply disappointed to discover that secondary school is nothing like he had hoped and, far from becoming one of the 'quality', he finds himself mocked by some of the other boys for his poor background. He admits that his own snobbery doesn't help him here and he realises later in life that if he hadn't made it so obvious he was ashamed of his poverty, the bullies would probably have left him alone.

Well-read, intelligent and quick with words

Jack is an avid reader and claims that his love of literature compensated for his learning 'next to nothing' in secondary school. He has a quick wit and uses this to defend himself against school bullies. His ability to deliver deadly insults soon makes him a 'crowd-pleaser' and he responds to this popularity by never missing an opportunity to make mocking and sarcastic comments, even if those he mocks make him suffer for it.

Can use his education and verbal agility to be cruel

Jack's intelligence and higher level of education than either of his parents gives him a certain arrogance in his teens. He does not yet have the maturity or the confidence to refrain from showing off whenever he gets a chance. When his mother asks him to write to his father's old employers to thank them for his pension, the sixteen-year-old Jack cannot resist making a literary allusion in what should have been a rather formal letter. Rather than simply do as his mother asks and mention that he has finished school and is looking for work, Jack compares himself to an unemployed character in a Dickens novel who is always hopeful that 'something will turn up'. Jack's mother does not understand this literary reference, and Jack makes it obvious that he thinks he is cleverer than her and that even explaining the reference would be a waste of time. When Jack's mother insists that he rewrite the letter, telling him to 'do it proper', Jack rather spitefully corrects her grammar. After a bitter argument, he does as he is told but ends the letter in a way that would be appropriate if he were writing a short note to a shopkeeper. His father is not sufficiently educated to realise what Jack has done and evinces delight at his son's work.

In a similar vein, Jack uses his sharp tongue and his quick wits to best a harmless old local man, Tommy Martin, who enjoys hanging around with Jack and his friends. Tommy is a rather pathetic figure who craves admiration and respect. He tries to make himself look important by 'dispensing unasked-for advice' and behaving in a domineering manner towards the young men. Jack's friends are tactful and understanding, but Jack admits that he lacks 'their in-bred tact and tolerance', and cruelly puts Tommy in his place. He realises later on that his behaviour was unfair and that he was 'using a sledgehammer to kill a gnat'.

Has a cynical view of patriotism

Jack was born four years after Ireland gained its independence from Britain, so the memory of the struggle for freedom was fresh in the minds of his parents' generation. As a young boy, Jack, like all his friends, is 'infected with the rabid nationalism' of the older generation. The words 'infected' and 'rabid' suggest that Jack regards such fervent patriotism as akin to an unpleasant disease. He also says that the fight for freedom was 'rather grandly called the War of Independence'. Clearly, he does not believe that the war merited such a title, which again indicates his lack of sympathy for the republican cause.

Nicholas Keyes

Jack's father

Hard-working, loyal and uncomplaining

Jack describes his father as 'a born provider' who works hard to take care of his family. He sees nothing unusual about working ten hours a day for the Jacobs and even boasts to his cronies that he has 'the best job in the country'. He has a fierce, almost familial loyalty to the Jacobs and persuades himself that they are generous to a fault. When he is given his Christmas bonus each year, Jack's father is so overcome by Mr Jacob's generosity that he announces brokenly that his employer is 'the decentest man that ever trod shoe leather'. He even finds it in himself to be grateful for the twisted lump of burnt spectacles that he is presented with on his retirement and expresses no disappointment that this worthless gift is accompanied by a sum of £25 instead of the hundred that might have been expected.

Nothing the Jacobs do is wrong, in Jack's father's eyes. When Mr Jacob reprimands him for forgetting to give him back a halfpenny change after being sent on an errand, Jack's father is neither insulted nor annoyed. Instead, he is delighted with Mr Jacob's words of wisdom: 'Half-pennies make shillings, shillings make pounds and that is why I am sitting where I am and you are standing where you are.' Jack's father repeats this to anyone who will listen, saying happily, 'And begod, wasn't he right?'

Loving, selfless father

Everything Jack's father does, he does for his family. He gives them his time and his money and asks for nothing in return. Jack recalls with great warmth the evenings spent walking around Dalkey with his father, yet when he abandons these walks and evenings at home in

hard-working
loyal
uncomplaining
loving
selfless
uneducated
class-conscious
sentimental
naive
amusing

favour of spending time with his teenage friends, Jack's father does not mention it, unlike his mother, who makes him feel guilty for drifting away from his family and towards independence.

When Jack needs a new suit for his post in the civil service, his father gets a second job in the evenings to pay for it. Jack can see that the extra work is exhausting his father and he feels guilty. However, when he tells his father that he does not want the money for the suit and that he should spend it on himself, his father is genuinely astonished at the thought. Despite his poverty, he believes that he has everything he could ever want and his only wish is to give his son all he can.

Uneducated

Even as a young boy, Jack is aware that his father is not well educated. Indeed, Jack's father has 'barely the schooling to write out a betting slip'. At that time it would have been very common for people from Jack's father's social class to finish their education at primary school level.

On their evening walks around Dalkey, Jack's father points out local places of interest to his son. One of these is a cottage in which George Bernard Shaw used to live. When young Jack asks who Shaw was, his father gives a vague reply that suggests he does not know.

Jack says that his father is 'the last person I would normally ask for information or advice'. On one occasion Jack does break his own rule and approaches his father to ask what 'adultery' means, but his father confuses 'adultery' with 'dilution'. Young Jack is satisfied with the explanation at the time and it is only some years later that he realises his father did not know the difference between the two vaguely similar words.

Class-conscious

Jack's father may have supported the War of Independence but he retains an attitude of respect towards what he regards as the 'quality': those who had been members of the ruling class during his youth. He admires the Jacob family and views Mr Jacob with awe. By contrast,

Jack's father is most unimpressed with the people who buy Enderley when Mr and Mrs Jacob die. The new owners are Catholics who are keenly aware of their recently elevated position in society. They regard Jack's father with suspicion as they have come from a similar background to his. They check his work and hint that he is taking advantage of them. Jack's father has no respect for these *nouveau riche* upstarts and he bemoans their lack of manners.

Positive and easy to please

'He was the kind of man who thanked God for a fine day and kept diplomatically silent when it rained.' This is the essence of Nick Keyes, a man who sees the best in everything and ignores that which does not fit into his positive view of his life. Jack describes his father as 'the most easygoing man alive'. Jack's mother wonders how her husband would respond to genuine good luck, such as winning the Sweepstakes. Her opinion is that such good fortune would be too much for him, considering how delighted he is with what little he has.

> *'He was the kind of man who thanked God for a fine day and kept diplomatically silent when it rained'*

Even the bleakest scenario does not seem to dampen Jack's father's good humour. When the government hands out gas masks during World War II, Jack's father says that 'neither dog nor divil' will escape the effects of the war and then laughs happily 'as if he could not wait to be blown sky-high'.

Sentimental

Jack's father is easily moved to sentiment, particularly when he dwells on how lucky he is to have such a loving family and such a wonderful job. The author describes his father almost shedding tears of gratitude as he dwells on how 'happy and contented' he and his loved ones are. However, there is a difference between this easily expressed sentiment and deeper emotions. The author claims that his parents, like many Irish people, enjoy 'the sentimentality of old songs because we confuse loose tear ducts with soft hearts'. Romantic ideas of love would not have come easily to Jack's father, who was of a generation which believed that such behaviour was best left to the upper class and to characters in books. For people of Jack's parents' class, simply ensuring that they had enough money to feed their family would have been uppermost in their minds. This is not to say that Jack's father did not love Jack's mother, but he would have found it difficult to say so.

Can be roused to passion

Jack's father is generally a mild-mannered man who is quick to believe the best of others, but when he feels his family is under threat he can fly into a rage. Jack recalls the time he was bitten by a dog and his father was so worried that he literally jumped up and down in a fit of temper. On another occasion, Jack sees his father becoming enraged on learning that his wife is planning to visit the home of her old admirer, Ernie Moore. There is no hint of any impropriety in the proposed visit, and it is only because Jack's mother has met Ernie's wife that there is talk of her calling to their house for tea. However, Jack's father will have none of it and says that he will not be responsible for his actions if the visit takes place. This is young Jack's first indication that his father truly loves his mother and is still capable of great jealousy when he thinks she might meet a man she cared for over forty years ago.

> Jack's father will have none of it and says that he will not be responsible for his actions if the visit takes place

Figure of fun

Jack describes his father as having an image of himself that is far removed from the reality, and he claims that the result can make him appear comical. He describes how his father won a turkey one Christmas. Instead of proudly coming home with an oven-ready bird under his arm, Jack's father is chased down their road by a 'very live and infuriated turkey', which attacks him with beak and claw. The neighbours who had gathered to see his triumphant return with his prize are highly amused by this sight. One elderly lady tries to pretend to Jack that the whole thing is an act designed to entertain the watchers, but young Jack knows better.

Even Jack's mother is aware that her husband, though a decent, hard-working man, is not always taken seriously and can appear foolish. For this reason, she instructs him to remain quiet and let her do all the talking when Mr Drumm visits the house to meet Jack. Naturally, Jack's father is 'not able to sit quiet if it killed him' and almost immediately brings up the subject of the war. His views make him appear ridiculous, although he has no idea that this is the case, and he is soon holding forth with his ill-formed opinions about Hitler and Churchill. When they are alone in the pub a short time later, Mr Drumm tells Jack that his father is ignorant but colourful and amusing. Jack's father would be shocked to hear this as he believes that he and Mr Drumm have a good relationship.

Politically naive

Jack's father's politics are based on his dislike of the English. He had supported the fight against the British in the War of Independence but had not been involved in any action. However, he is left with a lasting dislike of the British. When World War II breaks out, he claims to be on the side of the Germans but that is only because he views Hitler as the man who will put the English in their place. He hopes that the Germans will win and that, when they do, they will remember that the Irish remained neutral in the war and will reward the Irish people with jobs.

Margaret (Doyle) Keyes

Jack's mother

loving mother
passionate
insensitive
stubborn
manipulative
dominant
practical
class-conscious

Loving mother

She may not always show it, but Jack knows his mother loves him dearly. Both she and Jack's father do their utmost to ensure that Jack is well taken care of. Tiny details in the book show us Jack's mother's affection for her son. When he and his father go for their evening walks with the dog, Jack is 'half-choked' by the scarf his mother wraps around him. The scarf could be seen as a metaphor for Jack's mother's love. She ties it around him because she cares about him and wants to protect him from the elements, but he is constricted by the scarf and, by extension, by his mother's love.

Quick to anger/bears grudges

It is not just when she has had a few drinks that Jack's mother can lash out verbally. If Jack crosses her she responds instantly, sometimes in a very hurtful way.

Jack says that, like all the Doyles, his mother has 'a skin like tissue paper' and takes offence at the slightest insult, real or imagined. She falls out with her sister Chris because Chris fails to mention that they are sisters when introducing her to a friend. Jack's mother suspects, probably correctly, that Chris is ashamed of her sister's poverty and does not want to be associated with it. It takes many months before Jack's mother is prepared to forgive this slight and Chris is not allowed inside the door of the Keyes' house until Jack's mother has recovered sufficiently to let bygones be bygones.

Unpleasant when she drinks

Jack's mother likes a drink but alcohol has a bad effect on her. Jack says that when she has drink taken she is unpredictable and 'she would go for you if you vexed her'. Early in the novel the author tells of a family outing that ends badly when Jack's mother becomes drunk and aggressive, verbally abusing strangers when she suspects them of slighting her. Jack's mother does not drink regularly and when she does, she does so secretly. In time, Jack learns to recognise the signs that his mother is drinking and he takes it upon himself to find the miniature bottle of whiskey hidden in her handbag and pour the drink away. By the time Jack is in his late teens, his mother drinks even less frequently than she did when he was young, but when she does succumb to what Jack calls 'her weakness' the results are as detrimental to the Keyes' family life as they ever were.

Has the upper hand in her marriage and is the real head of the household

Jack says that he doubts if his mother ever thought of her husband romantically. That is not to say she does not love him, but he certainly loves her more. His father approached her parents and asked them to arrange the marriage, and they did, even though Jack's mother was going out with another young man at the time. Jack's father was a better catch because he had a steady job working for the Jacobs, so the match was made and Jack's mother informed of it in due course. This fact, combined with her determination and his easygoing nature, gives Jack's mother power over her husband. She does not consult her husband when she decides to adopt Jack, simply bringing the baby boy home with no warning. Less important, but in much the same way, some years later she brings home a stray dog, again without consulting Jack's father. In both cases, he accepts the situation stoically, knowing that she will have her way no matter what.

> She does not consult her husband when she decides to adopt Jack, simply bringing the baby boy home with no warning

Jack says of his father's relationship with his mother that he 'might strut and bluster, but it was she who ruled the roost'. When a policeman says that the family dog must be put down for biting a nun, Jack's mother overrules her husband's objections and insists that he have the animal destroyed. When the attempt to drown the dog fails, Jack's father is nervous lest she berate him for not carrying out her instructions, but she is delighted to see the dog returned to her and it is allowed to live with the family until the end of its days. It is not just in relatively unimportant issues like the fate of a pet that Jack's mother holds sway. It is she who decides that Jack should enter the civil service, and once she has made up her mind, the deed is as good as done.

Passionate, stubborn and manipulative

Jack finds it difficult to break away from his mother's control when he reaches adolescence. He describes her as 'a woman of passion who let nothing and no one go from her easily'. Like her mother (Jack's grandmother) she enjoys playing the role of the martyr. If Jack displeases her, she says nothing but affects such an air of reproach that no words are necessary. For this reason, Jack keeps secrets from her. For example, he never tells her that he takes a drink because he is sure that she would make him feel dreadfully guilty about doing so.

Practical

Jack's mother is far less sentimental and far more practical than her husband. When Mr Jacob dies, Jack's father is grief-stricken, but his mother focuses on the practical aspects of the situation, wondering if Enderley will be sold and if Jack's father will be out of a job. She does not have her husband's unquestioning devotion to the Jacobs and views them simply as her husband's employers, not as part of her extended family.

Class-conscious

She may not share her husband's devotion to the Jacobs but Jack's mother is nonetheless respectful to those from a higher social class than her own. When young Jack visits the wealthy Pearson family to give their son a present of sweets in return for all the sweets they have given him each Christmas, Jack's mother is appalled. She tells Jack that he has brought shame on the family and that the Pearsons will think they do not know their place.

Although she may be keen to show that neither she nor her family has ideas above their station, Jack's mother is less inclined than Jack's father to accept her lot in life. She enjoys 'mixing with well-off people and proving she is a match for the best of

'mixing with well-off people and proving she is a match for the best of them'

them'. When an old acquaintance invites her to tea at the Royal Marine Hotel, she is thrilled to sit among well-dressed, well-off women and she feels she is 'as good as the best of them'. She is even delighted when she is addressed as 'madam' by the waiter in the hotel.

Terrified of authority

Jack's mother dreads falling foul of the law or of the clergy. To be in trouble with either is to bring shame on your family, and such shame will not quickly be forgotten by the local community. When a local policeman calls to the house to follow up a complaint that the family dog has bitten someone, Jack's mother is deeply distressed and agrees to have the dog destroyed, even if that means upsetting her husband and son. It is not just the prospect of public humiliation that frightens Jack's mother; her fear of the law is described as deep-rooted and 'beyond argument or reason'. This may be because she is poorly educated and therefore has little, if any, understanding of legal matters. It may also be because she associates legal authority with an oppressive regime and, to a certain extent, sees those in power as the enemy.

Jack tells us of a time early in his parents' marriage when their home was raided by the Black and Tans who, correctly as it happened, suspected Jack's father of hiding weapons. Such a terrifying experience would be bound to leave Jack's mother with a fear of authority, particularly of those in uniform.

Insensitive to Jack's feelings about his adoption

Jack's mother regards Jack's adoption as her own story and does not consider how revealing it might affect her son. At that time, taking on an unwanted child would have been seen as an act of great selflessness and Jack's mother enjoys hearing people tell her how wonderful she is for rearing the boy as her own. Without considering the implications it might have for a boy starting in a new school, Jack's mother tells the adoption story to the principal of Presentation College. Jack realises: 'She could no more keep it to herself than she could stop from blessing herself when passing a chapel: it was her way of showing off what a great woman she was.'

On one occasion this insensitivity verges on cruelty. Stung by Jack's correction of her grammar when she orders him to rewrite his letter to Mrs Pim and to 'do it proper', Jack's mother begins to bemoan having adopted a boy who has now turned against her. Jack is sick of hearing the old story of how his mother took him in against all the advice of friends and family, and in his irritation he tells her to 'play another record'. Infuriated, Jack's mother lashes out by saying that Jack might pretend to be a gentleman and might think he is better than his parents, but he is not. She says that at least she and her husband are legitimate, unlike Jack. This seems an extraordinarily hurtful thing to say, and Jack admits that it is many years before he realises that 'love turned upside-down is love for all that'.

'love turned upside-down is love for all that'

Sonny Doyle

Jack's uncle

Lazy

Jack's uncle Sonny is an idle man who spends his time in the betting office, the pub or the dole office. He courts a woman called Kate Fortune but continues to live at home and only marries Kate when his mother dies. When it comes to contributing to the household income, he is no more use to Kate than he was to his mother. Since Kate has a job, Sonny sees no reason why he should change the habits of a lifetime, so he continues to draw the dole and Kate continues to toil away in the Dargle Laundry.

lazy
bitter
angry
paranoid
hypocritical
resentful

Fond of drink

The pub plays an important role in Sonny's life, along with the betting office and the dole office. He has a limp, which Jack's father claims was caused when Sonny fell asleep in the lavatory when he was drunk. Although Jack doubts that this is the reason for Sonny's limp, he knows only too well that Sonny is perfectly capable of drinking himself unconscious. Jack remembers once finding Sonny drunk, unconscious and standing upright with his head stuck in a hedge.

Bitter, angry and paranoid

Sonny believes that he has been denied 'a fair crack of life's whip'. It does not seem to occur to him that his refusal to stop drinking or start working might be to blame for his lack of success. He is convinced that people are only waiting for the opportunity to cheat him out of his due and he looks at the world with 'dark, disappointed eyes'. Sonny's bitterness makes him quick to anger, and he takes offence at the slightest perceived insult. He holds a grudge and if someone should forget to salute him, their name is 'scrawled indelibly in the black book of his brain'. In this readiness to make an enemy of anyone who crosses him, Sonny is like Jack's mother and all the rest of the Doyles. The author describes him as spending his nights 'dreaming of old hurts and new enemies'.

Hypocritical

When his mentally disabled sister Mary runs off to spend the day at the funfair, Sonny becomes convinced that she has been abducted and murdered. He is so consumed with grief that he does nothing to help in the search of the area, but remains at home, wailing about his 'lovely sister'. Mary is far from lovely, but it suits Sonny to play the role of the protective brother, which means little in practical terms beyond having a few drinks and wrongly accusing a harmless local man of being responsible for Mary's disappearance.

> it suits Sonny to play the role of the protective brother, which means little in practical terms

Sonny resurrects the image of himself as a loving brother some years later when his mother dies and Mary goes to live with Jack's family. Even though he is 'glad to see the last of her' because he can now get married and bring his new wife into the family home, Sonny tells anyone who will listen that his 'poor afflicted sister' was 'stolen' from him. He even writes a letter to that effect to Jack's mother, although he doesn't sign it. In typically paranoid fashion, Sonny believes that he can keep out of trouble with the law by never putting his name to anything.

Begrudges others their success

Sonny is deeply suspicious and resentful of anyone who appears to have a better life than he does. For this reason, he is predisposed to dislike his sister Chris's boyfriend, John Bennett. The author says that Sonny always tries to find a weakness in any new acquaintance so that he can feel superior to them. His detective work into his future brother-in-law's character reveals little, so Sonny is in a bad mood when he is first introduced to John Bennett. He is momentarily cheered on discovering that John Bennett is prematurely bald and makes a mocking comment about the other having a 'fine head of skin'. His enjoyment of the situation is short-lived, however, as he is put in his place by John Bennett's quick response: 'My hair simply fell out [...] Like your teeth.'

When Sonny hears of Jack's scholarship to secondary school, he offers no congratulations but hints instead that it was a sort of low cunning that got Jack the scholarship rather than any actual intelligence.

Mary Doyle

Jack's aunt

*cunning
child-like*

Neither as simple nor as angelic as she appears

Mary has 'the mental age of a seven-year-old' and is Jack's grandmother's pet. Jack is far from sure that Mary deserves the angelic status she is awarded at home, as he has heard her curse violently when taunted by local children, and he has been on the receiving end of many of Mary's sneaky and vicious punches. If he complains or cries out, Mary affects an attitude of such innocence that Jack is punished both for lying and for 'tormenting the afflicted'. Unsurprisingly, Jack seems to have little fondness for Mary and describes her unflatteringly and rather cruelly as 'a great shapeless lump of a woman' who skips home from her trips to the shop 'like a carefree young hippo'.

'a great shapeless lump of a woman'

Cunning

Jack's scepticism seems to be rewarded when Mary steals £2 from her mother and takes the tram to the funfair, where she spends the day. There is consternation in her absence, and when she returns, having cunningly kept aside just enough money for the fare home, Mary is scolded vociferously by Jack's grandmother.

Christine (Doyle) Bennett

Jack's aunt

Ambitious and determined

ambitious
determined
devoted wife

Chris Doyle is determined from an early age to escape the poverty into which she was born. She cultivates a more refined accent than the rest of her family and behaves far more demurely than them or any of her neighbours. She keeps herself to herself (the author describes her as 'a bird-alone') and she never allows the local boys to take liberties with her. Her attitude does not make her popular with the local women, who believe that she thinks too highly of herself, but she is not trying to impress them. She has set her sights on higher things.

Keen to reinvent herself and to shake off the traces of her old life

Chris succeeds in getting a job in a hat shop in Dublin and begins to move in slightly more elevated social circles than the other local girls. She ensures that the different groups of friends do not mix and takes her Sunday walks in Dun Laoghaire, where nobody knows her. She meets and marries John Bennett, a civil servant, and goes to live in a house 'with stairs in it and coloured glass around the hall door', sure signs that she has at last ascended from her family's labouring background to the relatively giddy heights of the lower middle class. When she marries John, Chris does her best to keep her old life separate from her new life.

> When she marries John, Chris does her best to keep her old life separate from her new life

Although she spends time with her family, Chris never lets them mix with the friends she has made since she married. An example of this can be seen when Jack is around thirteen years old and his aunt Chris is hospitalised. Jack's mother goes to see her and her visit coincides with that of another lady. Chris does not introduce Jack's mother as her sister as she is ashamed to be connected to somebody so poorly dressed and so obviously working class. She wants to remain in contact with her family, but does not want them to meet her new friends. She has placed herself in an almost impossible situation. The author says that it is as if Chris lives 'on top of a wall that was built too high to be seen across'.

In later years, Chris and John's habit of keeping to themselves and behaving like 'exiled royalty' earns them the local nicknames of 'The Duke and Duchess of Windsor'.

Devoted wife

Chris and John Bennett do not have any children but lead a happy life together in their perfectly organised home. The author says that Chris is a 'tireless wife' who ensures that every aspect of her husband's life runs like clockwork. The house is spotless, John's slippers are waiting inside the door for him when he comes home from work, and if he should get so much as a cold he is fussed over and nursed with the greatest of care.

John Bennett

Jack's uncle-in-law

Gentlemanly

When Chris meets John Bennett for the first time (on one of her Sunday afternoon promenades along the East Pier in Dun Laoghaire) she is immediately impressed by him. He is a civil servant and, although not in a senior position, he works regular hours and wears a suit on weekdays. He is polite and courteous to Chris, calling her 'Miss Doyle' and generally treating her like a lady. This is naturally attractive to Chris as she seeks to better her situation and rise above her working-class background.

John Bennett's manners and sense of decorum even survive his first introduction to his future in-laws. Chris is worried that he might be put off by her humble family home and by her mother and siblings. John, however, is admirably indifferent to everything from Sonny's thinly veiled insults to Mary's overly affectionate approaches. He is better able to cope than Chris could have hoped.

Not all he seems

John Bennett is not quite as perfect as he may first appear. For all his courtesy and gentlemanly behaviour when he talks to Chris, he is renowned in work for his use of bad language when anything goes wrong. This habit has earned him the nickname 'Curser' Bennett and his friends and colleagues are well aware that if John is stirred to emotion (particularly when he has drink taken and the conversation turns to politics) he is liable to fall into his old ways. Chris becomes aware of John's predilection for swearing and soon manages to put a stop to it

> For all his courtesy and gentlemanly behaviour when he talks to Chris, he is renowned in work for his use of bad language when anything goes wrong

in her quiet, calm way. However, the damage is done as far as promotion is concerned and John's behaviour in the office before he was tamed by marriage costs him any chance of promotion.

Happily married/devoted husband

At the time the author is writing the book, he still sees his aunt Chris and Uncle John regularly. They conduct themselves like 'exiled royalty' and seem very happy together, as they always have done. They have no children but live a sedate and orderly life in their perfectly run home.

Mrs Doyle

Jack's grandmother

Unpleasant and intimidating

Our introduction to Mrs Doyle (Jack's maternal grandmother) is not a positive one. She is a described as an obese, mean-spirited old lady who enjoys making all those around her fully aware of her poor health. She gives the impression that she is at death's door and even manages to intimidate her doctor into agreeing that she will not live much longer. She derives great satisfaction from the admiration of those who believe that she is a 'great old warrior' to have lived to such a great age, and ensures that everybody knows about her suffering by wheezing loudly and making as much noise as possible as she moves around her two-room cottage.

Mrs Doyle is the absolute ruler of the tiny cottage that she shares with her daughter Mary and son Sonny. Sonny has a fiancée, Kate Fortune, who is barely tolerated in Mrs Doyle's house: the elderly woman views Kate as a rival and the 'heiress presumptive to the cottage'. Sonny and Kate court for thirty years and only marry when Mrs Doyle dies. At that stage, the 'lovers' are in their mid-fifties.

unpleasant intimidating

Poor self-awareness

Mrs Doyle is a dreadful cook who produces fatty, burnt food and has no idea that her meals are anything less than delicious. Young Jack dreads mealtime at her cottage as it means eating fried eggs that taste like old rubber. He eats what is put in front of him as quickly as possible, fearing his grandmother's disapproval, but this only leads her to believe that her cooking is a success and she immediately begins to make more of the

> Mrs Doyle is a dreadful cook who produces fatty, burnt food and has no idea that her meals are anything less than delicious

same for her grandson. Her confidence in her culinary powers leads her to insist on cooking a meal for her prospective son-in-law, John Bennett, when she hears that he has a delicate stomach and can only eat light, bland food. She forces a greasy tea of sausages, rashers and left-over cabbage on him, believing that her common-sense methods will prove right and that John will realise the error of his ways. Of course, he is violently ill after eating such unsuitable fare, but Mrs Doyle does not hear about this as it occurs after he has left the house. It seems unlikely, given her powers of intimidation, that anyone would tell her the truth.

Mr Drumm

Jack's superior in the civil service

cold
forbidding
blunt
misanthropic
touchy
intelligent
arrogant

Middle class

Although he only features in the last two chapters of the book, Mr Drumm is an important figure in Jack's life. He works in the civil service and has the trappings of the middle class: a house with a name, not just a number, and a suit that marks him out as an office worker rather than a labourer. Jack's parents invite him to the house as they hope that he will write Jack a reference that will secure him a position in the civil service.

Cold and forbidding – not an easy man to approach

Mr Drumm's physical appearance is an early indication that he is not an easy-going, warm person. He is 'as thin and stiff as a hatstand', perfectly turned out, and with a smile that signals no warmth or happiness but is rather a private, bitter, mocking smile which seems to say he should have known better than to trust the person to whom he is speaking.

Insensitive

The first words Mr Drumm speaks in the book are to refuse Jack's mother's offer of a cup of tea and then, when she insists on his having one, to rather rudely chastise her for her foolish generosity. He is equally brusque with Jack, instantly correcting his speech and telling him to say 'yes' instead of 'yeah'.

When he and Jack go to the pub for a drink, Mr Drumm brings up the topic of Jack's adoption. He ignores Jack's obvious distress at having the subject raised and goes on to advise him to use his 'bastardy' to his advantage by having it 'light a fire' underneath him. He insists that Jack tell him his birth name as he will have to use that in the civil service. When Jack reluctantly admits that he is called John Byrne, Mr Drumm cruelly calls it a common name and says, 'Someone seems to have lacked imagination. Or can't have been bothered.' In what may be a clumsy attempt to console Jack, Mr Drumm tells him that he could have an 'unblemished' birth cert but still be as ignorant as his foster father. It does not appear to matter to Mr Drumm that he has now insulted both Jack's adoptive parents and his birth mother.

Misanthropic

Mr Drumm is a true misanthropist: he dislikes people in general. He speaks scathingly of almost everyone, from his colleagues to his own wife and family. His fellow countrymen who speak Irish are dismissed as 'clodhoppers and fanatics'; Jack's father and his ilk are 'inoffensive, stupid and not a damn bit of good'. Mr Drumm speaks of his daughters in equally disparaging terms, likening them to Rhode Island Red hens, hardly a flattering comparison.

Quick to take offence, slow to forgive

Although Mr Drumm does not balk at offending others, he does not forgive those who insult him. Anyone who challenges or irritates him is swiftly dealt with. A clerical officer who stands up to Mr Drumm on the matter of timekeeping is immediately moved to another branch of the civil service. It is not only those who work for him who are subject to Mr Drumm's 'venomous tongue'; he regards any interference from his superiors in the civil service as 'a battle cry', and should anyone be so rash as to meddle in the way he runs his office, he lashes out in a voice full of anger, loathing and contempt. Although this ensures that he and those who work for him are left alone, it does Mr Drumm no favours with those in authority and he is eventually transferred to an office where he works alone and has no opportunity to abuse his superiors or anyone else. Although this new post is ostensibly a promotion, it is obviously a way of getting rid of Mr Drumm and leave him with 'only deeds and dead files to tyrannise'.

Jack himself becomes one of the victims of Mr Drumm's displeasure. For reasons that remain a mystery, Mr Drumm takes against him one day and refuses to speak to him again, except to criticise him in front of his co-workers. Mr Drumm never forgives Jack for whatever it was he did to offend him, but when the time comes for Jack to leave the civil service in order to become a professional writer, he does seek out his old boss and makes his farewells. To his surprise, Mr Drumm is deeply moved by this news and even cries a little. Their 'old quarrel' is forgotten and they chat amiably before Jack takes his leave.

Some years later, Jack, now living in London, comes home for his mother's funeral and decides to pay Mr Drumm a visit. The older man is apparently pleased to see him, but his wife seems astonished to see her husband in a good mood. Jack has heard a rumour that she annoyed him some years previously and that he has not spoken to her since. Whether or not this is true, the fact that Jack can readily believe it says a great deal about Mr Drumm's difficult and unpleasant personality.

Intelligent but arrogant

Mr Drumm seems to believe himself superior to all those around him. He looks down on Jack's family and those like them, and he has little time for his colleagues or his own family. At work, he sees himself as a 'benevolent despot' who rules his section firmly but fairly. He is a religious man, but Jack suspects that he only goes to Mass in order to 'warn God to pull His socks up'.

'a formal and detailed critique of the play, written as if he were a professor to whom I, a student, had submitted a paper for marking'

Although he is not a writer himself, Mr Drumm does not hesitate to give Jack advice on his chosen profession. This belief in his superiority does not diminish once Jack becomes a successful playwright. In an act of kindness, Jack sends Mr Drumm tickets for his latest play and is rewarded with a letter containing 'a formal and detailed critique of the play, written as if he were a professor to whom I, a student, had submitted a paper for marking'. It is easy to see why Jack should call Mr Drumm 'an impossible man'.

Complex

It would be easy to dismiss Mr Drumm as simply arrogant and unpleasant, but there is more to him than that, though it is deeply hidden. He takes an almost fatherly interest in Jack and gives him what advice he can about life. Jack is not sure whether this interest is motivated purely by kindness or whether the fact that Jack is adopted leads Mr Drumm to believe that it is 'open season on strays', but whatever the reason, he appears to view Jack as a surrogate son. Jack fails to live up to Mr Drumm's expectations in this regard and incurs his displeasure for a reason that is never made clear to him. Instead of explaining, Mr Drumm simply cuts Jack off and treats him initially with hostility and later with indifference. Jack misses their friendship, if that is what the relationship could be called, but once Mr Drumm has made up his mind, there is little Jack can do to remedy the situation. Equally surprising is Mr Drumm's emotional response to Jack's announcement that he is leaving the civil service in order to write professionally. He is undoubtedly a difficult man to understand and his behaviour seems almost impossible to predict.

3

The single text

Guide to the Single Text exam section

Paper 2, Ordinary Level: this section is worth **60 marks**

The Single Text is the first section examined in Paper 2. There are a number of different single texts set each year and these are listed on the first page of your exam paper along with the relevant page number.

You are only required to study **one** of these single texts.

Beware: sometimes a book you are studying as part of your Comparative Study will also appear as a Single Text option. It is vitally important to answer the Single Text questions on *Home Before Night* only. If you use your Comparative Study text in the Single Text section, you will not be able to use it in the Comparative Study section.

You are required to know your Single Text in far more detail than you know your Comparative Study texts.

Because you are studying a novel rather than a play, you do not need to learn a large number of quotes. However, if you are hoping for a high grade, it would be no harm to familiarise yourself with some of the more important quotes from the novel. A good starting point would be to learn the quotes that appear in this book.

Types of questions asked

You will be required to answer **three ten-mark questions** and **one thirty-mark question**. There is no choice in the ten-mark questions; you must answer all of them. There is a choice between three different thirty-mark questions. You need only answer **one** of these.

Ten-mark questions

Character

This is undoubtedly the examiners' favourite type of question. You may be asked to comment on one or more of the main characters and say why they act the way they do in the novel.

Relationships

These questions generally focus on the central relationships in the novel, all of which are covered in detail in this book.

Plot questions

In these questions, you may be asked what happens at a particular point in the text. You must be accurate here. Do not give analysis or personal opinion when answering a question on the plot unless you are asked to do so.

The world of the text/social setting

You may be asked questions about the setting of the novel and how the time and place in which they live affects the characters.

Theme or issue

You may be asked to comment on the theme of the text.

An important moment in the text

You may be asked to describe a happy, sad, pleasant, disturbing, violent, frightening, important, amusing, enjoyable or dangerous moment. Remember, when describing this moment, to say **why** it is happy or sad, etc.

The ending

You may be asked to comment on the ending. Was it what you expected? How were things resolved for various characters?

Writer's attitude towards the subject of the novel

Be sure you are able to say what this attitude is and how it is conveyed to us by his writing.

Thirty-mark questions

Many of the questions in this section are similar to the ten-mark questions. The principal difference is the length of answer expected. This type of question is effectively a short writing task, similar to the Comprehension Question B answers on Paper 1. You should bear this in mind when planning and writing your answer. The **layout** of the letter or diary entry or whatever you may be asked to do is not as important as it is in the Comprehension Question B section, but if you are looking for a high grade, you should make an effort to use appropriate language, show an awareness of your audience and generally show an understanding of how such a task should be approached.

As it is a thirty-mark question, you should be aiming to write around six paragraphs, each containing a valid point.

There is an element of personal response here, but be very careful to ensure that your answer is based on the novel. There is occasionally some scope for you to use your imagination but only in the way you express yourself. In other words, if you are asked to pretend you are one of the characters and are writing a diary entry after a significant event, you must be sure to stick to the facts of the event as they are presented in the novel. This is a test of your knowledge of the novel. Don't be fooled by seemingly vague questions or by the word 'imagine'. The answers must all be based on the Single Text itself and nothing else.

If you are asked for your opinion of the novel, try to be positive. You may not like the book but it was chosen as a good example of its genre, and you would be unwise to criticise it.

Character study

This is a very common question, as it is in the ten-mark section. In this question, you may be asked to pretend you are one of the characters in the novel, and to write the diary entry he or she might make after a significant event. Or you may be asked whether or not you could live with one of the characters. Another option may be a question requiring you to write a speech defending or prosecuting a certain character Of course, the question may simply ask you to analyse one of the main characters, but it is more likely to be framed as a short writing task along the lines of those given in Comprehension Question B on Paper 1.

World of the text/setting

You may be asked what differences there are between the world of the text and the world in which you live. Would you like to live in the world of the text? What have you learnt about the world of the text from reading the novel? How did the setting/world of the text affect the plot and/or the characters' lives?

Relationships

These questions generally focus on the central relationships in the novel.

Review

You may be asked to write an article or a speech in which you give your opinion of the novel. In general, you will be asked to present this speech or article to an audience of your peers. In other words, you should be prepared to tell other students what you thought of the book and whether or not you would recommend it to them. Make sure to consider several different aspects of the novel when planning your answer. Is the theme one which would appeal to your peers? What about the language? Does the book move at a fast pace and keep you gripped from start to finish? Are the characters likeable? Could you relate to the issues dealt with in the novel? Did you learn anything from the novel?

Try to be as positive as you can when answering this question. Refer to the novel in every single paragraph.

Report

Here you will have to imagine that you are a reporter or possibly a police officer, writing a report on an event that has taken place in the novel.

Theme or issue

What view of life do you get from the novel? Is it uplifting or depressing? Are there life lessons to be learned? What is the author's attitude towards the theme of the novel?

An important moment in the text

You may be asked to describe a happy, sad, pleasant, disturbing, violent, frightening, important, amusing, enjoyable or dangerous moment. Remember, when describing this moment, to say **why** it is happy or sad, etc.

Alternative endings

Occasionally, you are asked to imagine how the events in the novel might have turned out if characters had made different choices. This is a difficult question to tackle as the temptation to wander far from the text itself can be great. Try to base your answer on the text insofar as it is possible to do so. Try to keep the characters' behaviour in keeping with the way they have acted throughout the novel.

Important note

The Comparative Study notes in this book are also intended to be used to help Ordinary Level students prepare for the Single Text section of the examination. For example, **themes**, the **world of the text** and **relationships** are also dealt with in the Comparative Study section and all of these are areas which should be covered by anyone studying *Home Before Night* as a Single Text.

Guidelines for answering exam questions

This section is worth **60 marks** and should take
you a little less than an hour to complete

When you read the question, underline the key words: **describe,
explain, outline,** etc.

Study the question carefully. Try to paraphrase it. What exactly are
you being asked? Is the question on plot or character, for example? Is
there more than one part to the question? Look for the word 'and'. This
can be an indication that there are two parts to the question.

Plan your answer. It is well worth taking the time to do this.

Think in terms of key moments: this will ensure that you refer to the
text and will help you to keep the sequence of events in the right order.

Do not, under any circumstances, simply summarise the plot.

Remember that, as a general rule, (although you must be guided by
the question first and foremost) five marks equals one well-developed
point. One well-developed point equals one paragraph. So, if a question
is worth thirty marks, you should try to make at least six points. You
may also wish to include a brief introduction and conclusion.

It cannot be stressed enough that, unless you are specifically asked
to do so in a recall question, simply retelling the story will not get you
marks. Avoid falling into the trap of simply describing the world of the
text without saying what effect it has on the characters' lives.

In order to get high marks, you need to:

- *Answer the question asked (30 per cent).*
- *Make sure every paragraph develops that answer (30 per cent).*
- *Use varied and appropriate language (30 per cent).*
- *Keep an eye on your spelling and grammar (10 per cent).*

Look back over the plan. Does each point you are intending to make
answer the question? Is each point backed up by an example from the
text? Do the paragraphs flow logically from one to the other?

Past examination questions

Paper 2, Ordinary Level

2005 **C.** *Home Before Night* – Hugh Leonard
      Answer **all** of the questions.

1. (a) Give a brief description of an incident in *Home Before Night*
    that you found enjoyable and say why you found it so. Refer to
    the text to support your answer. (10)

    (b) From your reading of *Home Before Night*, how did Hugh
    Leonard feel about attending secondary school? Refer to the text
    in support of your answer. (10)

2. Describe one important difference between the way of life as
    described in *Home Before Night* and life in Ireland today. (10)

3. Answer **one** of the following: [Each part carries 30 marks]

(i) Many memorable characters (mother, 'da', aunts, uncles, family
     members, neighbours, friends, etc.) are portrayed in *Home
     Before Night*. Which one of the characters did you find most
     memorable? Explain your answer with reference to the text.

                              OR

(ii) 'The novel, *Home Before Night*, shows us that family is important
     in all our lives.'
     Write a short speech that you would make to your classmates on
     the above topic. Refer to the novel in your speech.

                             · **OR**

(iii) The editor of a magazine, whose purpose is to encourage young
      people to read, has asked you to recommend a book to its young
      audience. You decide that your choice will be *Home Before
      Night*. Write the review that you think will sell *Home Before Night*
      to the magazine's young readers. Refer to the text to
      support your views.

Sample answers

1. (a) Give a brief description of an incident in *Home Before Night* that you found enjoyable and say why you found it so. Refer to the text to support your answer.

2005 **10** MARKS

Comment: You could describe the incident first and then say why you liked it, or you could mix the description and the comments together, as in the answer below. Either option would be fine.

An excellent answer will give more than one reason for liking the chosen section.

When you are saying why you **liked** a section of the book, you could consider some or all of the following: effective characterisation; a turning point in the plot; humour; sadness; tension; excitement; use of dialogue to add dramatic effect.

SAMPLE ANSWER 1

An incident in *Home Before Night* which I found enjoyable was the occasion when Mr Drumm visits the Keyes' house in order to meet Jack and write a reference for him. The visit is vividly described in a way that shows us the mixture of hilarity and sadness that marks so much of Jack's childhood.

Jack's father is wonderfully portrayed in all his naive eagerness to please. Jack's mother has instructed him to be quiet and to leave all the talking to her as she fears that he will say something foolish and alienate the prickly Mr Drumm. Naturally, Jack's father is 'not able to sit quiet if it killed him', and soon puts his foot in it by holding forth with his ill-formed beliefs about the war and expressing his support for the Germans. Mr Drumm is not impressed and Jack's mother is tense as she senses his disapproval. Jack's father is undeterred and carries on praising Hitler while denouncing Winston Churchill as 'a yahoo with a cigar stuck in his fat gob and a face on him like a ... a ... a boiled shite'.

The opening paragraph outlines the events and gives the main reasons for liking this particular incident. The rest of the answer will describe the incident in more detail and develop the reasons for finding it enjoyable

When discussing dialogue, quotes are a great help

This dialogue adds greatly to the humour of the incident as we can almost see Jack's father struggling to come up with the best way to describe Churchill and settling on a crude expression that will undoubtedly do little to win over the steely, disapproving Mr Drumm.

Adding to both the tension and the hilarity is the sound of Jack's 'mad aunt Mary' upstairs, banging her pramful of dolls into the wardrobe in a fit of temper. She has been banished lest she embarrass her family but she still manages to make herself heard.

Links between paragraphs (using words such as 'although') help to ensure that your answer is well structured

Although it contains much to amuse, the visit is not without its sad moments. Once again, Jack has to cope with his mother telling the story of his adoption. He overhears her coming to the end of the tale when he arrives downstairs with the civil service forms for Mr Drumm. I could appreciate Jack's sinking feeling on realising that the detested story would now follow him from school to his work place.

It is important to show a personal response to the question asked. In other words, you must explain why you related to a character or found something amusing or poignant, for example

While I enjoyed all of *Home Before Night*, this was undoubtedly my favourite part and even now I smile as I think of the final moments of the visit: Jack's father snapping into a Nazi salute and nearly knocking Mr Drumm's hat off while his mother clings to Mr Drumm's stiff arm and tries to wheedle him into giving Jack an excellent reference. As I see this scene played out in my mind's eye, I also see an awkward, resentful young man striding down the garden, away from the embarrassment of his family and towards a future career in which

Even in a ten-mark answer, you should write a brief conclusion

he has little say and even less interest. It is a beautifully drawn sketch of family life and of all the mixed emotions that are an inescapable part of growing up.

10 MARKS   **2005**   1. (b) From your reading of *Home Before Night*, how did Hugh Leonard feel about attending secondary school? Refer to the text in support of your answer.

Comment: This is a ten-mark question, so you should aim to write at least two paragraphs in your answer. You may also wish to include a brief introduction and conclusion. Try to structure your answer logically. For example, you might discuss the difference between what the author hoped secondary school would be like and his disappointment when he found that it was nothing like his dream. Then you could move on to discuss the time he spent in Presentation College and how he got on with the staff and his fellow pupils.

Remember to focus on the way the author felt about school. Use plenty of words to describe his feelings: hopeful, excited, anxious, disappointed, resentful, frustrated, bored, frightened.

The question refers to the author's pen name, Hugh Leonard, but you can refer to him as 'Jack' or 'Hugh Leonard' in your answer.

Support each point you make with reference to a specific incident in the text, if possible.

Chapters 8 and 9 of *Home Before Night* deal with the author's time in secondary school. You should re-read these chapters before writing your own answer to this question.

SAMPLE ANSWER 2

The author's time in secondary school was a disappointment to him educationally and socially. He had high expectations before starting in the Presentation College, but these hopes were soon dashed.

The opening sentence sets the tone for the rest of the answer

An avid reader of *The Magnet* and its stories of English public school life, the author was delighted when he won a scholarship to attend a prestigious secondary school. In his mind, this school was just like the fictional Greyfriars School in *The Magnet*. Young Jack longed to be like one of the heroic 'Chaps' in those stories and he felt sure this was his chance to realise his dream. In addition, he looked forward to the chance to reinvent himself and to escape what he saw as the stigma of his illegitimacy.

The answer shows detailed knowledge of the events described in the book and also answers the question by mentioning how the author felt about these events.

The reality was not at all what the author had imagined. For a start, he was dismayed to discover that his mother told the principal, Brother Berchmans, the story of Jack's adoption. Things did not improve on Jack's first day when the other boys mocked his father's shabby appearance. Embarrassed and ashamed, Jack punched the boy

Note the use of words that describe feelings: dismayed, embarrassed, ashamed, etc

who asked if that could really be his father. Instead of being one of the popular 'Chaps', Jack realised miserably that he was in fact like one of the 'Bullies' in the Greyfriars stories. His humiliation was intensified later that day when Brother Berchmans decided against giving him raffle tickets to sell, as he was worried that Jack might steal the money he raised. It was at this moment that Jack realised just 'how far away Greyfriars was'.

Short quotes help, but if you are unsure of the exact wording of the quote, simply refer to that part of the book instead, using your own words

Although there were some kind teachers and some humorous moments during the author's time in secondary school, his overwhelming experience was one of unhappiness. He learned nothing there and only achieved a measure of popularity by learning to use his wits to mock others. He made no lasting friendships and was tormented by a gang of boys who mocked his poor background. Added to this misery was the corporal punishment meted out regularly by the teachers and the principal.

Brief conclusion reflects the wording of the opening paragraph and ties up the answer neatly

All of these experiences combined to make the author's time in secondary school miserable and unproductive. He achieved little and repeated the same year twice until his scholarship ran out, after which he left the Presentation College 'without a backward glance'.

10 MARKS | **2005** | 2. **Describe one important difference between the way of life as described in *Home Before Night* and life in Ireland today.**

Comment: When you are preparing to answer this question, you should read the section on Cultural Context/Social Setting in the Comparative Study section of this book. You could choose any one of the areas covered in this section and discuss it in your answer.

Remember to focus on the word **difference**. You are not asked to comment on any similarities between the way of life in the novel and life today.

Some of the issues you could write about in your answer are education, family life, sense of community, financial status of Irish people, religion.

In your answer, you should concentrate on the text rather than going into too much detail about life today. If you choose to discuss education, give examples from Jack's primary and secondary schooldays as evidence of, for example, the frequency with which corporal punishment was used. You would not be expected to give examples from your own experience of education, but you should comment briefly on the fact that this method of punishment is not only unacceptable but also illegal in today's educational system.

SAMPLE ANSWER 3

One of the principal differences I noticed between the way of life as described in *Home Before Night* and life in Ireland today is the way pupils were treated in schools during the thirties and forties.

The opening sentence makes it clear what topic has been chosen

In the novel, Jack describes his experiences in both primary and secondary school. I was struck by the strict discipline meted out in the three schools he describes. An example of this can be seen in Jack's description of an incident that took place when he was a young boy attending the Loreto Convent. His pen slipped and rolled down his exercise book, leaving marks on the clean page. Although this was not Jack's fault, he was punished for it by his teacher, Sister Ita. When Jack's father complained about the unfairness of this, Jack was punished again by the same nun, this time for telling tales. I do not think that today's pupils would readily accept such unfair, strict, authoritarian discipline.

The answer goes through Jack's schooling in chronological order. This is an easy way of ensuring that the answer is well structured

Things did not improve for Jack when he moved on to Harold Boys' School. His first teacher, Alfie O'Hagan, squeezed the hands and ears of the boys he liked but with 'the dodgers and mitchers he used his cane and his fist'. The headmaster, Tabac, was a quick-tempered man who slashed at the boys with a cane he kept under his desk. Tabac was especially furious with any boy who misbehaved when Father Creedon visited. In today's Ireland a pupil would certainly not be beaten for offending a member of the clergy or anyone else.

Brief quotes show a good knowledge of the text

Each paragraph ends with a comparison between education in Jack's time and education today

When Jack won a scholarship to the Presentation College, he soon found that life in that school involved the same strict discipline he had experienced in his other schools. He recounts the 'loosening of the bowels' that accompanied an instruction from Brother Berchmans to wait outside the door for a beating. The aspect of corporal punishment that seems strangest to me is the boys' ready acceptance of it. The author recalls one lay teacher who did not beat the boys and was therefore regarded by the pupils as 'weak'. This would certainly not be the case today.

Brief conclusion ties up the answer neatly

All in all, I am very glad that I received my education in twenty-first-century Ireland rather than the Ireland of the thirties and forties.

30 MARKS **2005**

3. (i) Many memorable characters (mother, 'da', aunts, uncles, family members, neighbours, friends, etc.) are portrayed in *Home Before Night*. Which one of the characters did you find most memorable? Explain your answer with reference to the text.

Q. *What sort of task is this?*
A. This is a persuasive piece.

Q. *What should the content be?*
A. You can choose any character you like; there is no right or wrong answer. What is important is that you make a strong case for finding your character memorable. Once you have selected a specific person, read the notes on their character (Chapter 2). Decide which five or six traits you are going to discuss. They can be positive or negative or a mixture of both. Each point about the character should be supported by reference to a specific moment or moments in the novel.

As the question calls Jack's father 'da', it would be appropriate to do so in your answer if you wish.

Q. *Who is my audience?*
A. There is no audience specified in this question. If this is the case, then try to imagine you are writing for your own teacher, and err on the side of caution. You will not be penalised for being too formal in

your writing, but you may be penalised for using a chatty tone when it is inappropriate to do so.

Q. *What register should I use?*

A. See above.

SAMPLE ANSWER 4

The character in *Home Before Night* that I find most memorable is Jack's father. He comes across as a kind, decent, funny man who adores his wife and child and has an admirably positive attitude to life.

The opening paragraph outlines the points that will be made about Jack's father in the rest of the answer

Da, as young Jack calls him, is a loving father and spends a good deal of time with his son. The evening walks the pair take around Dalkey when Jack is a young boy are recounted with affection and warmth. As they stroll, Jack's father tells his son the history of the places they pass. He is not an educated man but he is keen to impart what knowledge he has. On one of their walks, Jack admits to being afraid his birth mother will come and steal him away. His father comforts him by making up a story about her living far out to sea on the Kish lightship and goes on to assure Jack that, if she should turn up one day, he will give her 'the biggest root up the arse a woman ever got'. The description of that particular walk stays with me because it shows how caring and protective Jack's father is.

Each point is supported by a brief description of a key moment in the text, and linked back to the question by phrases such as 'stays with me'

His utterly selfless nature is one of the other traits that makes Jack's father unforgettable. As Jack grows older, he spends more time with his friends and less time with his family. In contrast to Jack's mother, who makes her son feel guilty for seeking his independence, Jack's father allows him the freedom he desires and demands nothing in return. At the same time, he continues to work long hours to provide for his son as best he can. When Jack needs a new interview suit, his father immediately goes out and finds extra work in order to earn the necessary money. One of the most striking images in the book must be of the now elderly man coming home from his second job, exhausted, carrying his scythe over his shoulder and looking 'like the old year going out'. And yet, when Jack tries to persuade him to spend the extra

Links between paragraphs make your answer flow well

money he has earned on himself, his father dismisses the notion out of hand, claiming that he and Jack's mother are 'grand, wantin' nothin' from no one'.

Another aspect of Jack's father's character that I find particularly memorable is how amusing he is. An incident which clearly shows how hilarious he can be, albeit unwittingly, is the occasion on which Mr Drumm visits the house to give Jack a reference for the civil service. Although he has been warned by his wife to say nothing lest he embarrass them, Jack's father is characteristically 'not able to sit quiet if it killed him'. He holds forth with his ill-formed political opinions, claiming that the Germans will win the war and will have 'lashin's of grand jobs' for their friends, the Irish. Happily unaware of the disapproval of his listeners, he goes on to describe Winston Churchill as being 'a yahoo, with a cigar stuck in his fat gob and a face on him like a ... a ... a boiled shite'.

Short quotations from the novel help to show the examiner that you have a good knowledge of the text

Although he is exceptionally entertaining and easy going, Jack's father has a passionate side to his character, even if it rarely comes to the fore. In fact, the only time we see evidence of it is when he hears that Jack's mother intends to visit her old boyfriend, Ernie Moore. To Jack's shock, his father loses his temper and rants and rages, becoming almost violent in his fury. He doesn't seem to care that it is over forty years since his wife and Ernie went out together or that Ernie is now a married man. In his temper, he smashes his pipe to pieces on the range. This incident stands out in my mind because it shows the depth of Jack's father's feelings for his wife and proves to us, and to Jack, that he is capable of strong emotion on occasion. Indeed, it makes such a strong impression on Jack that he retrieves and keeps the broken pieces of the pipe.

I think the lasting memory I have of Jack's father is his overwhelmingly positive approach to life. Jack describes him as the sort of person who 'thanked God for a fine day and kept diplomatically silent when it rained'. This positivity is all the more striking when we consider how difficult his life is. The family is far from well off, yet Jack's father believes that they want for nothing because they have a home, enough to eat and one another. In this materialistic age, such an attitude should give us pause for thought. Jack's father may lack education but he possesses qualities that are far more important than any qualification.

There are many fascinating characters in *Home Before Night* but none of them made as strong an impression on me as Jack's kindly, optimistic, sometimes ridiculous, always loving father.

Brief conclusion reflects the opening paragraph and refers back to the question

---

3. (ii) 'The novel, *Home Before Night*, shows us that family is important in all our lives.' Write a short speech that you would make to your classmates on the above topic. Refer to the novel in your speech.

2005 30 MARKS

Q. *What sort of task is this?*
A. This is a speech to your classmates.

Q. *What should the content be?*
A. While you are not specifically told to agree with this statement, it would be wise to do so. Remember, 'the importance of family' is not necessarily the same thing as 'the wonderful influence of family'. You can say that Jack was occasionally adversely affected by his relationships with his parents, but still acknowledge the importance of this in his life.

Q. *Who is my audience?*
A. Your audience is people of your own age.

Q. *What register should I use?*
A. You are addressing people of your own age, so your language can be quite relaxed and informal if you wish. However, you should remember that this is an English examination. Avoid excessive use of slang, and under no circumstances use text language. If in doubt, err on the side of formality in your writing. No examiner will penalise you for being overly correct.

SAMPLE ANSWER 5

A brief, chatty introduction is appropriate for a speech to your classmates. This is not a formal, debate speech

Good morning, everyone. As you know, or should know, it's Father's Day on Sunday, so Mr O'Connell suggested that I talk to you about Hugh Leonard's *Home Before Night*, a text we all know well after two years of study, and explain why I think it shows the importance of family in all our lives.

When I think about this book, the first thing that comes to mind is the wonderful character creation, and how so much of that is centred on the author's family. The detailed description of Jack's grandmother in the first chapter will stick in my mind for a long time. I can clearly see the 'vast, malevolent old woman, so obese that she was unable to wander beyond the paved yard outside her front door'. And who can

Remember, this is a question on the text. Occasional, short quotes are a good idea

forget Aunt Mary, skipping down the road 'like a carefree young hippo'? Okay, these may not be the most flattering descriptions in the world, but I think they prove how important these people were to young Jack, in that he can recall them with such devastating clarity so many years later. And of course there are the touching details about Aunt Chris and John Bennett's courtship and marriage. The author's keen knowledge of the lives of members of his family makes me guiltily aware that I know nothing like as much about my own family. In fact, after reading that chapter I asked my parents how they met. They were fairly surprised I was interested, I have to say!

You were asked to talk about the importance of family in 'all our lives', so you should link the points to your life and that of your classmates

One of the things I found most touching about the book was the relationship between Jack and his father. Even now, years after his father's death, the author can still remember their evening walks together, the little boy holding his dad's hand which was 'as rough as tree bark'. Jack's dad was not an educated man, but nevertheless he taught his son valuable life lessons. Da worked uncomplainingly to provide for Jack and his mother, and never asked for anything in return. I suppose, if we're honest, we all take our family for granted a little bit, never really stopping to think how much they do for us. If the book makes us consider that for even a moment or two, then that's no bad thing.

Of course, not all Jack's memories of his family are happy ones. I'm sure we can all relate to his occasional embarrassment at having to be seen in public with his parents. Admittedly, he had good reason to be embarrassed when his mother made a drunken spectacle of herself on the *Royal Iris*, but there is less excuse for his shame when his fellow pupils sneered at his father in his working clothes. One of the unhappiest memories Jack has is of his mother's repeated references to his illegitimacy. It hurt Jack deeply when his mother used it as a weapon in a particularly bitter argument, and he admits that it was years before he learned that 'love turned upside-down is love for all that'. I think what this shows us is that our family relationships affect us deeply, even if it's sometimes in a negative way.

Link every point to the topic

The ending of the book sums up the importance of family in the author's life. He is returning to Ireland to live, having spent some time in England. As he drives back into Dublin, he remembers 'another journey home, long ago'. In his mind's eye, he sees a little boy rushing through the gathering darkness of evening, hurrying towards his parents, who are waiting anxiously for him. He describes the little cottage as 'the two lighted rooms that were the harbour at world's end'. I think that it is no harm for us to think about that for a moment, and appreciate the fact that anyone who has a loving home to go to is lucky indeed.

Thank you for listening so patiently, and I hope I have given you some food for thought.

Be sure to provide a definite ending to your speech

3. **(iii) The editor of a magazine, whose purpose is to encourage young people to read, has asked you to recommend a book to its young audience. You decide that your choice will be *Home Before Night*. Write the review that you think will sell *Home Before Night* to the magazine's young readers. Refer to the text to support your views.**

2005 30 MARKS

Q. *What sort of task is this?*

A. This is a review. You should be familiar with this type of task from your preparation for the Comprehension Question B section of Paper 1. Your aim is to get young people to read the book, so you should use the language of persuasion. Again, you will have studied this language genre when preparing for the tasks on Paper 1.

Q. *What should the content be?*
A. This is a review, so you should include an introduction, description, evaluation and recommendation.

Q. *Who is my audience?*
A. Your audience is any young person reading the magazine. It would be safe to assume that the age range would be mid to late teens. The examiners generally tend to ask you to write for people around your own age.

Q. *What register should I use?*
A. You are addressing people of your own age, so your language can be quite relaxed. You should also note the audience: in this case it is young people, so your language can be reasonably informal. However, you should remember that this is an English examination. Avoid excessive use of slang, and under no circumstances use text language. If in doubt, err on the side of formality in your writing. No examiner will penalise you for being overly correct.

SAMPLE ANSWER 6

The tone of the introduction is quite chatty, as would be appropriate for a magazine

When I was asked to choose a book I would recommend to the readers of this magazine, I wondered where on earth I would find a book that everyone would enjoy. The answer, when it came, surprised me as much as it might surprise you. There, among piles of exam papers and dull textbooks on my desk, was the perfect choice: Hugh Leonard's *Home Before Night.*

The readers are addressed directly; this is a feature of persuasive writing

So what's it all about? Well, the basic story is quite simple. *Home Before Night* is Hugh Leonard's autobiographical account of growing up in Dublin during the thirties and forties. We follow Jack's journey through his childhood, adolescence and early adulthood.

Jack's situation is one with which any teenager can easily identify. He loves his parents but, as he grows up, he finds their love for him restrictive, irritating and embarrassing. For example, Jack's first day in secondary school. He has won a scholarship to Presentation College and views this as a chance to break free of his poor background and an opportunity to reinvent himself in the mould of one of his heroes of script or screen. That is something we can all remember to a greater or lesser extent: the desire to make a good impression, to keep our heads down until we know the lie of the land, and to make the most of a fresh start. Picture, then, young Jack's mortification on realising that not only has his mother told the principal the whole story of his adoption, but his father is fully intent on accompanying him to school on the first day, dressed in his working clothes with 'caked clay on his half-mast trousers' and boots 'bent like the rockers of a cradle'.

A brief description of the plot is given

Reasons given for liking the book are linked to the audience

One of the things that I found most enjoyable about this book is the humour that permeates almost every page and brings the characters so vividly to life. The description of Jack's father is a classic example. He is a wonderfully optimistic man who, when gas masks are handed out during World War II, says that 'neither dog nor divil' will escape the effects of this war, and then laughs happily 'as if he could not wait to be blown sky-high'. On the other end of the scale is Mr Drumm, Jack's intimidating boss in the civil service. But even he is described in such a way as to make the reader smile. His pomposity and unpleasantness are wonderfully captured from the moment he arrives at Jack's house and closes the garden gate, giving it 'a look of dislike that dared it not to stay shut'. Every character in this book is utterly captivating, whether it is because we love them or loathe them.

Examples from the novel back up the points being made

On a slightly more serious note, this novel captures the essence of a bygone era. It tells us of an Ireland in which our grandparents and great grandparents struggled to make their way. It was a time of financial and physical hardship. For example, you may find it difficult to believe that not so long ago it was considered normal for young people to have all their teeth removed and replaced by a false set, but that was very much the case in Jack's time. His friend Joe has all his pulled when he is twenty and is delighted with the result, claiming that whenever he has a toothache now, all he needs to do is take his teeth out and put them on the dresser. It is a measure of the author's skill that he can make such a story amusing.

Evaluation   *Home Before Night* is a hilarious, engaging, entertaining, captivating, coming-of-age story and an unforgettable description of a time that is a part of the heritage of all Irish people. I cannot recommend this book highly enough and I urge those of you who have not read it to do so at the earliest opportunity. You won't regret it, trust me.

---

30 MARKS   **SAMPLE QUESTION**   'The relationship between Jack and his mother is a complex one.' Do you agree or disagree with this statement? Explain your answer with reference to the text.

Q. *What sort of task is this?*

A. This is a persuasive piece.

Q. *What should the content be?*

A. You should try to think of five or six reasons why the relationship is complex. An easy way to approach this is to start at Jack's early childhood and move through the years up to his adulthood. As he grows up, his relationship with his mother naturally changes.

If you agree that the relationship is a complex one (and it would be hard to argue differently) then be sure to include a mixture of positive and negative elements. These do not need to be balanced; you may have two negative points and three positive ones, for example.

Q. *Who is my audience?*

A. There is no audience specified in this question. If this is the case, then try to imagine you are writing for your own teacher, and err on the side of caution. You will not be penalised for being too formal in your writing, but you may be penalised for using a chatty tone when it is inappropriate to do so.

Q. *What register should I use?*

A. See above.

SAMPLE ANSWER 7

I believe that Jack's relationship with his mother is a complex one. He loves her but he resents certain aspects of her treatment of him. As is so often the case in relationships between parents and children, the balance between this love and resentment tips different ways as Jack grows up.

The opening paragraph addresses the question and states the viewpoint that will be supported by the rest of the answer

As a young boy, Jack has quite a good relationship with his mother. He is an adored only child and his mother does her utmost to take good care of him. There are occasional lapses, such as the occasion when she becomes drunk on a family day out and embarrasses her son, but even in these difficult moments Jack consoles himself with memories of happier times. He recalls his mother taking him to not one but two Santas at Christmas and then treating him to lunch in Pim's restaurant. This would have been an extravagant treat and one his mother could ill afford.

Key moments from the text are used to illustrate each point made

When he reaches his teenage years, Jack begins to spend less time with his family and more time with his friends. His mother tries to make him feel guilty for this but Jack knows that underneath it all she is enjoying the role of wronged mother. His reaction to this is to lie to her 'like a trooper' and attempt to play her at her own game. He justifies this by saying that if he were to stand up to her openly, he would not stand a chance. Jack appears torn between amused respect for his mother's ability to fight and resentment at her refusal to simply let him go.

One aspect of his relationship with his mother that causes Jack a great deal of distress is her habit of telling people about his adoption. She shows enormous insensitivity in this and does not seem to care that it is a sore point for Jack. On one occasion Jack and his mother fight over whether or not he should rewrite a letter to his father's former employers, and her trump card is bringing up his illegitimacy and saying cruelly that at least she and his father know 'where they were got and how they were got'. Years later, Jack realises that 'love turned upside-down is love for all that', but as a teenager he is understandably incapable of taking such a reflective approach to his mother's dreadfully hurtful remark.

Part of the problem that Jack has with his mother is the contrast between the expectations she has for his future and his own hopes and dreams. Because she comes from a poor, working-class background, Jack's mother believes that Jack would be doing extremely well if he, like his uncle John, were to get a job in the civil service. She manages to convince a reluctant Jack to apply for the post, persuading him that 'the pension and the three pounds fourteen a week' is worth it. Jack is bitterly unhappy in the civil service but does not entirely blame his mother, accepting that he gave in to the pressure she and his aunt put on him 'because Yes was always easier to say than No'. There would be little point in his trying to explain to his mother that what she sees as a wonderfully secure post, he sees as a dead-end job. Although Jack loves his mother and she him, they see the world quite differently, which creates tension in their relationship.

Overall, however, I think that Jack has a good relationship with his mother, despite their ups and downs. The final image in the book is the author's memory of himself as a seven- or eight-year-old boy, running home to his parents as evening falls. He fondly imagines that he can see his mother waiting anxiously, 'one hand comforting the other' as she peers down the lane to see if he is on his way. There is great affection and warmth in this description and the love Jack feels for both his mother and his father is clear when he says that, for him, the small two-roomed cottage was 'the harbour at the world's end'.

4

The comparative study

Home Before Night

In this chapter you will find comprehensive notes on using *Home Before Night* as a text for your Comparative Study. Each of the comparative modes for Higher Level and Ordinary Level is covered. As the modes change each year, it is important to check which modes apply to the year you will be sitting your Leaving Cert.

Some of the modes for Higher and Ordinary Level overlap. Where this is the case, one set of notes is given for the two modes.

It is very important to be able to compare the texts you are studying, but you should also bear in mind that at both Higher and Ordinary Level you will usually have the option of answering a thirty-mark question on **one** of the texts.

These notes are designed as a reference guide to help you put together your own Comparative Study essays. In some cases, headings are used for clarity and to make revision easier, but you should not use headings in your own answers.

There is a certain amount of overlap between the comparative modes, particularly in relation to key moments, but this is inevitable. A key moment can show aspects of the central relationship, the literary genre and the cultural context, for example. As you will only be answering on one mode in the examination, this overlap is not a problem.

In this book, key moments are woven into the Comparative Study notes. As a key moment is described, its relevance to the mode is discussed and explored in detail. Remember: never discuss an event in your chosen text without linking it to the point you are making.

Important Note

The Comparative Study notes in this book are also intended to be used to help Ordinary Level students prepare for the Single Text section of the examination. For example, **themes, the world of the text** (cultural context/social setting) and **relationships** are dealt with in the Comparative Study section, and all of these are areas that should be covered by anyone studying *Home Before Night* as a Single Text.

Literary Genre

Higher Level

Past questions on this mode of comparison have tended to focus on the following:

- *How memorable characters are created in the text*
- *How emotional power is created in the text*
- *Aspects of narrative and how they contribute to your response to the text*
- *How powerful moments add to the story in the text*
- *How the unexpected contributes to the story*
- *The different ways in which the story is told in the texts you have chosen.*

Point of view

Unusually, the chapters in this novel alternate between first and third person narration. When first person narration is used, we hear the author's adult voice and are privy to his considered opinions on the events he recounts.

Hugh Leonard's wit, humour and sometimes devastatingly cruel characterisations shine through this first person narration. In the first chapter, his mentally disabled aunt Mary arrives home from a shopping trip 'skipping like a carefree young hippo and swinging a shopping bag which had probably disfigured any name-callers imprudent enough to venture within range', while his social-climbing aunt Chris 'made the most of her dark plumpness and cured herself of the adenoidal Dalkey accent which made two syllables out of one'.

Unusually, it is when he narrates in the first person that the author describes in imaginative detail events that he could not possibly have seen. He tells us that when his aunt Chris first met his uncle John, 'she felt as if she were a passenger on a tram and the conductor had called out the destination'. There is nothing in the novel to suggest that his aunt would have confided such intimate recollections to her nephew, so it is fair to assume that the author is giving us his own version of events that happened before he was born. Similarly, he tells us that his grandmother enjoyed the sympathy of those who believed her tales of ill health while 'privately, she saw no reason why she should go any time, but she liked to nod submissively, essay a practice death rattle and resignedly endorse the will of the Almighty'. Again, it is unlikely that the author's grandmother would have expressed such opinions to her grandson or to anyone likely to pass them on to him.

'she liked to nod submissively, essay a practice death rattle and resignedly endorse the will of the Almighty'

Third person narration can be objective and may allow the author to be omniscient (all knowing), but this is not the case in *Home Before Night* as we are only shown events from Jack's point of view.

When third person narration is used in the novel, it reflects the speech patterns and view of life that the author had during the various stages of his childhood and adolescence. For example, the second chapter, narrated in the third person, tells of an occasion when Jack, aged seven or eight, goes on a family outing which ends badly when his mother becomes drunk and aggressive. He is embarrassed by her behaviour but feels utterly helpless in his misery as he watches her arguing with strangers or confiding in them that she regrets adopting Jack. The language in this chapter is far simpler than the language in the previous chapter, and many of the sentences are quite short, as would be appropriate for a young boy. Even the similes used are ones that would make sense to a small child. An angry man on the *Royal Iris* is described as 'dribbling like a baby' in his temper, and the darkness of the night is 'black as a coal hole'.

The effect of this narrative technique is twofold. The third person narration encourages us to view Jack sympathetically as we see significant moments in his childhood from his perspective as a young boy or a sensitive teenager. The first person narration puts these events into context and allows the author to share with us the life lessons he has learned and the conclusions he has drawn from his various experiences.

Plot/narrative pattern

Home Before Night is an autobiographical account of Hugh Leonard's childhood in Dublin during the thirties and forties. Events are described in more or less chronological order, but there are a number of stories from the time before the author was born and these are woven into the narrative to help put certain anecdotes into context. For example, the occasion when Jack's father becomes enraged on hearing that his wife is planning to meet Ernie Moore (her boyfriend of forty years ago) is prefaced by a description of Jack's parents' arranged marriage, a marriage that ended Jack's mother's relationship with Ernie. Knowing the background to the story, the reader can more easily understand Jack's father's jealous fury at the mention of Ernie's name even after so many years have passed.

> The author's memories of growing up are not all happy. The very first story from Jack's childhood is of his mother's drunken anger ruining a family day out

The author's memories of growing up are not all happy. The very first story from Jack's childhood is of his mother's drunken anger ruining a family day out. However, among the sad memories, there are also many happy ones: trips to the cinema with his mother; walks around Dalkey with his father and the family dog; and happy Sundays spent enjoying the simple pleasures of lemonade with dinner and a new comic. These are just some of the times Jack recounts with affection.

Whether the events described are amusing or disturbing, the manner in which they are told captures the reader's interest throughout. The opening lines of the book are an example of how this is achieved. 'My grandmother made dying her life's work. I remember her as a vast, malevolent old woman, so obese that she was unable to wander beyond the paved yard outside her front door.' The author then draws us into his life by telling us amusing and revealing stories about his mother's family, the Doyles. These alone would be enough to encourage us to read on, but the ending of the chapter raises such an intriguing question that it would be almost impossible not to want to know more. Having told us that his aunt Chris and her husband are childless, the author startles us by stating, 'None of the Doyles of Chris's generation had children – including my mother.' Chapter 7 begins with the astonishing sentence: 'Two events marked my fourteenth year: I stopped going to confession and I killed Mrs Kelly who lived on our road.' It would be difficult for any reader not to want to discover the facts behind this statement.

> *'Two events marked my fourteenth year: I stopped going to confession and I killed Mrs Kelly who lived on our road'*

The author's attitude towards his childhood is a generally positive one, as is evidenced by the ending of the novel. Driving home again after several years spent living in England, the author remembers another trip home long ago when, as a young boy, he rushed towards the safety and warmth of his waiting parents and the 'two lighted rooms that were the harbour at world's end'.

Creation of characters

The characters in *Home Before Night* are, at times, larger than life. We rely on the author's omniscient narration and we are entirely dependent on him for our impressions of the various characters.

The depiction of the central characters (Jack's parents, for example) shows them in all their complexity, but the portrayal of the minor characters such as Father Creedon could be viewed as rather one-dimensional.

Hugh Leonard's genius in characterisation lies in his keen observation of detail and the effective and evocative metaphors and similes he uses in his description of each character. Brother

Berchmans, the thoroughly unpleasant principal of Presentation College, wears 'black robes that hissed like snakes as he walked'. When we read this, we can instantly sense the malevolence of the man and the threat of danger he carries with him wherever he goes. Brother Berchmans speaks in clipped tones, his words cut short 'as if with a nail scissors', hinting at a determined effort at self-control and (because of the reference to scissors and cutting) a sense of barely suppressed violence.

In contrast, we can see the author's love and concern for his ageing father when he describes him coming home after a long day at work: 'his tiredness and the scythe carried over his shoulder made him look like the old year going out'.

'his tiredness and the scythe carried over his shoulder made him look like the old year going out'

Jack's mother is undoubtedly a complex character. It is a mark of Hugh Leonard's skill that he manages to present her as both a loving mother and an insensitive, sometimes cruel parent. He achieves this by showing us the range of emotions he feels during various interactions with his mother. An honest narrator, Leonard does not shy away from showing us the negative aspects of his mother's character, but he also shows us how much he loves her and appreciates that she loves him too.

A good example of the author's portrayal of his mother's complexities is shown in Chapter 10, when Jack is ordered to rewrite the letter to Mrs Pimm, the daughter of his father's former employers. The teenage Jack resents his mother's lack of comprehension of his allusion to Dickens and does not see why he should have to change what he has written. His mother picks up on her son's attitude: he thinks she is too stupid and uneducated to understand his letter. The tension between mother and son escalates and Jack is instructed to 'write it out again and do it proper'.

The use of dialogue between mother and son in this section shows clearly the difference between their speech patterns, reflecting the difference in their educational backgrounds. Rather unwisely, Jack corrects his mother – 'properly' – and she promptly loses her temper. In a devastatingly cruel blow, she lashes out verbally, telling Jack that while he may look down on his parents, they are better than he is in one way at least: they are not illegitimate. Her fury and the loss of control that have led her to be so harsh are shown in the description of her shaking with temper while her 'fists, pressed down on yesterday's *Irish Press* that was the tablecloth, were bunched and white'. The detail about the newspaper used as a tablecloth is telling; it reminds us that Jack's mother is poor but that she has pride. She may not be able to afford a tablecloth but she will have one. This mixture of poverty and pride is part of what makes her so complex. On the one hand, she is proud of Jack's academic success because she feels he will be able to make more of his life than she managed with hers, but on the other hand she resents his making it clear that he has already outstripped his parents in terms of education. Combined with her quick temper and sensitivity (Jack says that she has 'a skin like tissue paper'), this inevitably leads to conflict with her son.

Whether the characters are sensitively portrayed or held up as caricatures of a certain type of Irish person at the time, there is no doubt that they are described in such witty, affectionate or bitingly humorous terms as to make them unforgettable.

Dialogue

The use of dialogue in *Home Before Night* adds greatly to the realism and the humour of the novel. A certain amount of dialect is used: enough for us to become familiar with the speech patterns and attitudes of the characters, but not so much that we are forced to slow down and re-read sentences. For example, Jack's father's innocence and ignorance is made clear in a conversation with Mr Drumm in which he claims that when the Germans win the war there will be 'good jobs handed out beyant in England'. The dialect word 'beyant' evokes the accent of a working-class Dublin man of that era, emphasises Jack's father's lack of education and thus takes the sting out of a speech in which Hitler is praised as a great man.

It is not just in humorous scenarios that dialogue is used effectively. Brother Berchmans' 'flat nasal voice' and habit of clipping his words 'as if they were cut with a nail scissors' is wonderfully captured in the novel, bringing the cruel principal vividly to life. The author remembers the sinking feeling in the pit of his stomach when Brother Berchmans signalled that a caning was imminent by instructing Jack to: 'Git ahtside the door, pliss. Ah'll be aht in a minnit.'

Social realism

Home Before Night is an example of social realism and an historically accurate depiction of life in Dublin in the thirties and forties. Life is hard for Jack's family and their ilk. He spends his early childhood in a two-room cottage with no indoor toilet. When it is cold, his parents use coats as extra blankets. The only real hope of escape from the poverty trap is through education, and Jack is fortunate enough to win a scholarship to attend secondary school. Without this scholarship, it is likely that he would have had to follow in his father's footsteps and go to work at an early age. His father was employed as a gardener for the Jacob family when he was only fourteen years old and continued to work for them for the next fifty-four years.

> The only real hope of escape from the poverty trap is through education, and Jack is fortunate enough to win a scholarship to attend secondary school

Popular culture

Young Jack is an avid reader of British schoolboy comics like *The Magnet* and from these he forms an idea of a perfect school, one in which the masters are strict but fair and the pupils divided neatly into 'Bullies' and 'Chaps'. He longs for an opportunity to become one of the 'Chaps' and is therefore delighted when he wins a scholarship to Presentation College, as he believes the school will be similar to the ones his fictional heroes attend. The reality is nothing like he had hoped, of course, and he is bitterly disappointed.

In an era before television and computers, the cinema plays an important role in the lives of Jack and his friends. Through their regular trips to see the adventures of Bulldog Drummond or Charlie Chan, the lads escape into another world. No matter how terrible the films, the boys watch them, 'eyes glazed like zombies, living any lives in preference to our own'.

General Vision and Viewpoint

Higher Level

Past questions on this mode of comparison have tended
to focus on the following:

- *How the general vision and viewpoint of a text is determined
  by the success or failure of a character in his or her efforts
  to achieve fulfilment*
- *How you came to your understanding of the general vision and
  viewpoint in your chosen text*
- *The way in which a key moment or moments can influence your
  understanding of the general vision and viewpoint of a text*
- *How the general vision and viewpoint is shaped by the reader's
  feeling of optimism or pessimism in reading a text*
- *Your understanding of the general vision and viewpoint
  in your chosen text*
- *What you enjoyed about the general vision and viewpoint of
  your chosen text.*

Home Before Night is a realistic portrayal of life in a working-class area
of Dublin in the thirties and forties. Woven into a series of memories
of his youth are the author's comments on the era in which he was
raised. He does not flinch from detailing sad moments in his childhood
and is critical of many aspects of Irish society, but the overall mood of
the book is positive, mainly because of the author's ability to see
humour in almost every situation.

The novel opens with the line: 'My grandmother made dying her
life's work.' This rather cynical comment sets the tone for the rest of
the chapter, in which the author introduces his mother's family.

Through his amusing, carefully selected anecdotes Hugh Leonard encourages us to view the Doyles as amusing or slightly ridiculous. There is much about which he could be pessimistic – poverty, death, unemployment, crime, alcoholism and mental disability – but the author presents these facts in such an entertaining way as to eliminate almost all traces of gloom. Even the mention of his grandfather's death has a hint of the ridiculous about it when we are told that he died suddenly 'after cleaning out a cesspit'.

The stories of family life the author chooses to share with us reflect his view of the world. They are a blend of happy, almost idyllic scenes of childhood and occasions of pain and sadness. Nostalgia is not permitted to dominate at the expense of realism. The walks around Dalkey with his father, perfect Sundays spent in the company of his family and trips to the cinema are described in

'a place of weeds, rusting cans and boy-made swamps where, when the sun came out, the earth blazed with broken glass'

loving detail, but even when recounting these pleasant memories of his youth the author maintains an unromantic view of life. He and his friends play contentedly in the lane outside their houses, but it is 'a place of weeds, rusting cans and boy-made swamps where, when the sun came out, the earth blazed with broken glass'. The perfection of an evening walk with his father is marred by young Jack's memory of his aunt's threats about his birth mother coming to take him away.

Just as the positive, almost sentimental descriptions of happy moments are tempered by the author's refusal to ignore the realities of life, so the unpleasant memories are lifted by notes of optimism and by the author's wry comments on events. When recalling a family outing that was spoiled by his mother becoming drunk and obstreperous, Hugh Leonard does not allow himself, or us, to wallow in the sadness of the occasion. The young boy's misery is somewhat alleviated by recollections of other, happier outings with his mother. Jack views the woman who tries to comfort him, as he stands on the quayside watching his parents argue with a stranger, not as a rescuer but rather as an irritation. Her attempts to remonstrate with his parents when they finally disentangle themselves from the quarrel are met with failure when his father sweeps Jack up 'the way a snowball would pick up a stone' and carries him off without breaking his stride. The author says admiringly that it was 'the sort of thing you could not do a second time if they paid you'. Even in the bleakest times in the young boy's life, there are moments of cheer.

The author's parents may not be perfect, but they are loving and supportive. They do their best for their son and he grows up in a largely nurturing environment, despite the family's lack of money. This is not to say that the author views family life entirely positively. He is frustrated by certain aspects of it, some of which are connected to his parents' personalities and some of which have to do with social issues. He cannot understand his father's lack of expectations for himself, and the older man's fawning admiration for the 'quality' angers young Jack. Nor can he easily accept his mother's frequent references to his illegitimacy. That she should mention it at all, and particularly in such a way as to distress her son, may seem extremely harsh to modern readers, but she is merely reflecting a common view at the time – that illegitimate children were somehow tainted and likely to turn on those foolish enough to take them in. The author's obvious distress and embarrassment at hearing her talk in such a manner is one way in which he shows his distaste for the prevailing attitudes of the era.

The author takes a dim view of some elements of mid-twentieth-century Irish life. He is scathing in his criticism of those who subscribe to what he calls the 'rabid nationalism' of the time and he mocks their sectarianism and ignorance. His parents and their neighbours watch indulgently as young Jack and his friends parade up and down chanting anti-English rhymes outside the house of a local man who has the misfortune to be pro-British. Later, he is disgusted and embarrassed by his father's support of Hitler during World War II, a support which the author claims is based less on any real political viewpoint than a dogged belief that any enemy of the British is a friend of his. The Catholic Church and the Irish education system are portrayed equally unfavourably, mainly through the rather one-dimensional portrayal of the majority of the teachers and members of the clergy. Father Creedon is an unsympathetic, pompous man who seems to have little compassion for his congregation, while Brother Berchmans, the principal of Presentation College, is depicted in such a manner as to make him appear a virtual devil. The language the author uses to describe Brother Berchmans hints at violence and misery: he has a 'long coffin-shaped face' and his smile is 'like a cut throat'. Even his clothes seem menacing: his robes hiss 'like snakes' as he walks. Neither priests nor teachers in *Home Before Night* are seen as having much interest in helping the author or any other characters in the novel to achieve self-fulfilment. Instead, their primary function seems to be to repress those unfortunate enough to be subject to their power. The author's attitude towards both is almost entirely negative and it is no surprise that he leaves school after fourth year, claiming to have learned 'next to nothing' there.

As he grows older, the author finds that his view of his home town and his family changes. He begins to long for freedom and finds less enjoyment in the pastimes of his early youth. He and his friends, now young men, spend their days at the seafront, but they are waiting 'to be set free from each other by marriage, a job, a twist of fate, a miracle'. The metaphors the author uses highlight his view that his life is stultifying and restrictive. The seafront is 'a treadmill' or 'an exercise yard' and they are 'short-term prisoners' who are hopeful of not having to serve a 'life sentence'. At home, Jack's mother does her best to make her son feel guilty for spending less and less time at home, but he finds humour even in this, describing her emotional manipulation affectionately and wryly.

The later stages of the novel, when the author joins the civil service, present us with the most negative view of his life. He does not share his mother's belief that a job in the civil service is so wonderful that anyone fortunate enough to have a position there is made for life. He loathes his job and feels nothing but sick misery at the thought of having to spend the whole of his working life in the civil service. On his first day, he reflects bitterly that he has worn new trousers 'to go into prison'. He is consumed by thoughts of escape but it is not until six months later that he sees any hope of an alternative future. His first trip to the theatre fills him with hope and joy and he sees at last the door he will escape through. However, even when telling us of his worst days in the Land Commission, the author does not lose his ability to see the absurd and the amusing in the characters around him. The descriptions of the hunchback Mr Hozier, who 'ran like a spider' around the office, and the rather unhinged Mr Kennedy, who would sit in silence for most of the day and then suddenly shout, apropos of nothing, 'I weighed meself this morning in the men's lavatory in Ballsbridge' or some similar inanity, lightens the tone considerably.

'I weighed meself this morning in the men's lavatory in Ballsbridge'

It is the ending of *Home Before Night* that gives us the greatest insight into the author's view of his childhood. He returns to live in Dublin several years after his parents have died. As he drives towards the city, he remembers when, as a boy of seven or eight, he found himself quite far from home one evening and was forced to run as fast as he could in order to be home before darkness fell. The final scene is of the author's parents waiting anxiously for him, his mother peering down the lane and his father checking the time. Everything in the little cottage is warm and welcoming. The tea is ready and waiting and the author envisions himself hurrying towards 'the two lighted rooms that were the harbour at world's end'. The reader is left with a sense of joy and optimism as the boy runs towards the love, security and comfort that await him.

Cultural Context

Higher Level

Social Setting

Ordinary Level

Past questions on these modes of comparison have tended to focus on the following:

Higher Level

- *The way in which the world or culture the characters inhabit affects the storyline*
- *The way in which the world or culture they inhabit shapes the characters' attitudes and values*
- *What is interesting about the world or culture of the texts*
- *How the author establishes the cultural context.*

Ordinary Level

- *What you liked or disliked about the social setting*
- *What you found interesting about the social setting*
- *The way in which the social setting influences the characters*
- *How a key moment can show us the way in which the social setting affects the characters.*

Setting

The author grows up in Dalkey, a coastal suburb of Dublin. Dalkey is Jack's world when he is young, and describing his father as 'the best da in the whole of Dalkey' is the greatest compliment he can think of. The setting of the novel has a profound effect on Jack. He lives in a small, close-knit community and there is a great sense of security associated with this. When he is very young, he plays happily on the lane and the waste ground outside his house, even though it is 'a place of weeds, rusting cans and boy-made swamps where, when the sun came out, the earth blazed with broken glass'. This and the other playgrounds of Jack's youth are described in affectionate detail, and each is linked to events and people of his childhood.

As Jack grows older, he begins to find the small community in which he lives more of a restriction than a joy. He longs to get away but fears that he may never escape and may, like his father, end up living the same life in the same place forever. Dalkey becomes like a prison for Jack. The metaphors he uses to describe the seafront ('treadmill', 'exercise yard') reinforce this idea, and Jack's only hope is that he and his friends are only 'short-term prisoners' in this place.

As Jack grows older, he begins to find the small community in which he lives more of a restriction than a joy

Political background

Jack was born in 1926 and grows up during a time of great political change in Ireland.

In *Home Before Night*, Jack tells of his father's republican sympathies and of the 'rabid nationalism' that was passed down to the children of those who lived through the War of Independence. As a young boy, Jack happily accepts his father's view of the world as it is one which is shared by his friends' parents too, but as he grows older he comes to see how naive and simplistic his father's political views are. For example, during World War II Jack's father sides with Hitler and the Germans on the grounds that his enemy's enemy is his friend. He shares his thoughts on what he sees as the inevitable German victory with Mr Drumm when the latter visits the house to meet Jack. Mr Drumm is unimpressed and Jack is keenly aware that his father appears ridiculous as he describes how Hitler 'druv them into the sea in nineteen-forty and he'll do it again now'.

Class distinction

The social class to which he belongs has a profound effect on Jack's life. His early childhood is spent in a two-room cottage in Dalkey. His father works long hours as a gardener, while Jack's mother is a housewife. Money is tight and Jack's parents' greatest ambition is that their son should be a success in life and escape the cycle of poverty into which they were born. Jack's aunt Chris has already succeeded in doing this by marrying a civil servant, John Bennett.

> Money is tight and Jack's parents' greatest ambition is that their son should be a success in life and escape the cycle of poverty into which they were born

There is snobbery even within the poor terrace of cottages where the Keyes live during these years. On one occasion, Johnny Quinn, a neighbouring boy from a family even poorer than Jack's, brings Jack with him to the door of another neighbour, Mrs Threadgold. Jack realises, too late, that Johnny has called on the woman in order to beg for food. Mrs Threadgold gives the young lads some bread and jam, and Jack is embarrassed and ashamed that he should appear to be 'no better than Johnny Quinn'. He knows his mother would be furious if she found out. Although the family is poor, her boast is that they 'paid their way, were under a compliment to no-one and never wanted for anything, least of all nourishment'.

Jack's parents, while espousing the values of independence and taking pride in owing nothing to anybody, have a strange respect for those they consider to be the 'quality'; people from a higher social class. Jack's father, in particular, has a great admiration for the remaining representatives of the old Anglo-Irish ruling class. Money alone is not enough to gain his respect. He adores the Jacob family, for whom he works for many years, and when they eventually die and the house is sold to a Catholic family, he is not impressed. He seems to resent the fact that he is now working for people he feels are in many ways no better than he is, and he dislikes their constant checking up on his work. He believes that working for people like himself (Irish Catholics) is nothing like as rewarding as working for old, established, wealthy families like the Jacobs.

The author shares his father's contempt for the newly rich members of Irish society. He feels that with the passing of the Jacobs and their like came a new breed of 'huxters and chancers' who lacked the style of those they replaced. He uses scathing language to describe these people: 'the gombeen men and their wives with backsides that sang of soda bread and spuds'. His father describes them in a typically direct way: 'whoor's ghosts'.

Jack's mother does not share her husband's respect for the members of the old order. Neither is she overly impressed with her sister Chris's affected airs and graces and adoption of a new, middle-class accent. Chris, for her part, is keen to distance herself from her working-class background. She is careful that her new friends never meet her family. The author describes her as being like someone who 'lived on top of a wall that was built too high to be seen across'. Chris's worst fears are realised when she is hospitalised with an illness and Jack's mother visits at the same time as a friend from Chris's new life. Chris manages to introduce the women without admitting that Jack's mother is her sister. This causes a rift between the two sisters that lasts for several months. Yet, even though Jack's mother complains about the Jacobs and grumbles about Chris, she is nonetheless keen for Jack to move up in the world.

The issue of class consciousness affects Jack's chances of achieving a good secondary school education. He wins a scholarship and his mother asks aunt Chris's advice over which school Jack should attend. She replies that he should definitely go to Presentation College because a better class of boy goes there. It is amusing that Chris, of all people, should label the boys who go to the Christian Brothers as 'a common crowd' who are merely 'letting on to be gentlemen'. After all, she is 'letting on' to be something she is not, and Jack's mother is fond of saying 'that to look at Chris you would think that she had never gone barefoot in her puff'.

'to look at Chris you would think that she had never gone barefoot in her puff'

On Jack's very first day of secondary school, he is made keenly aware of the class differences between him and his fellow pupils. The other boys spot Jack's father waving goodbye to him and instantly mock his poor working clothes and generally shabby appearance. Jack, embarrassed and ashamed, punches the boy who asks him if that 'horny handed son of the soil' is related to him. This damages Jack's chances of being accepted by the other students and of passing himself off as one of 'the quality'. Later that same day, the principal hands out raffle tickets to the boys so that they can raise money for the poor of the parish. Jack is perfectly willing to sell tickets but Brother Berchmans refuses to give

'We don't want to be led into temptation'

him any, saying: 'We don't want to be led into temptation.' To be so humiliated in front of the rest of the class does not embarrass or anger Jack as much as he might have thought. Instead, he feels like smiling as he reflects on his vanished dream of fitting in with the other boys and having the sort of upper-class experience of school that he has read about in his English comics. The reality is that he cannot escape his background, much as he might wish to. The other boys sense his snobbery and his shame at his family's poverty, and he becomes the 'prey of a small band of tormentors', one of whom regularly follows him home in an attempt to 'see for himself the meanness of the cottage I lived in'. Jack is so desperate to prevent the boy from succeeding in this enterprise and carrying the tale back to school that he walks around Dalkey for miles rather than going straight home.

Education

In 1926, the year Jack was born, the School Attendance Act made it compulsory for children between the ages of six and fourteen to attend school. The Department of Education also introduced the Primary School Certificate examination around this time. For many youngsters, this certificate was their highest qualification in education. Very few children went to secondary school when Jack was a boy, so his scholarship would have set him apart from the other local children. When his neighbour Mrs Costello hears that Jack is to attend secondary school, she announces stiffly: 'The national schools are good enough for my childer and sorry one of them the worst for it.'

Jack does not excel at secondary school and stays in fourth year for three years in a row until his scholarship runs out. The fact that he finishes school without a Leaving Certificate is not as much of a hindrance to Jack as it would be today. He gets a place in the civil service despite his lack of educational qualifications.

Jack does not recall his schooldays with any great fondness and claims that he learned 'next to nothing' in his years in Presentation College. His status as a scholarship boy sets him apart from the other boys and Jack makes no lasting friendships. Neither does he have anything positive to say about the majority of the teachers he encounters in either primary or secondary school. His memories are punctuated with descriptions of savage canings for relatively trivial offences.

For modern readers, the descriptions of the beatings Jack and the other children receive at the hands of the teachers are quite shocking. It must be remembered, however, that physical punishments were the norm in those days and the schools Jack attended were typical of the time.

Religion

The author's view of religion is largely cynical and unsympathetic.

When Jack's dog bites a nun, the horror of having offended a member of the clergy and at the same time having broken the law is almost too much for Jack's mother

Jack's mother's attitude is symptomatic of the prevailing attitude of Catholics of her class at the time. She views both the clergy and the police as dread figures of authority. They are best kept at a distance, and unwavering obedience to the rules of the Church and the laws of the country are the only certain ways of avoiding unnecessary contact with priests or policemen. When Jack's dog bites a nun, the horror of having offended a member of the clergy and at the same time having broken the law is almost too much for Jack's mother.

Jack's father has never forgiven the Catholic Church for excommunicating rebel fighters during the Civil War, and he is therefore furious when Jack falls foul of Father Creedon in confession one day and Father Creedon takes it upon himself to berate Jack's father for his son's shortcomings. Jack's sin was forgetting the words of a prayer (mainly due to his terror of Father Creedon) and this failing gives the priest the opportunity to 'lord it over' Jack's father by claiming that the family does not pray together regularly.

There is no sense in this novel that the clergy may have a kinder, more spiritual side. The Presentation Brothers Jack encounters in his years at secondary school are not particularly Christian in their attitudes. The students are beaten for any misdemeanour, and there is an implication that at least some of the clergy, particularly Brother Berchmans, may be using corporal punishment as a way of venting their own frustrations.

In later years the author and his friends regard the Catholic Church's main role as one of persuading young women that they should rebuff their boyfriends' attempts at physical intimacy. Rather cynically, the author believes that elderly members of the congregation encourage the priests to preach about the hellish torments that await those who indulge in 'carnal enjoyment' because they are past the age when they can enjoy it themselves, and gain satisfaction from the younger generation also being deprived of sexual pleasure.

> As an adult, he is surprised to see that the tormentors of his boyhood are nothing more than old men who take an almost childish delight in slipping and sliding around on the ice in the schoolyard

Several years after he leaves school, the author becomes a relatively successful writer and he is invited back to his old school to help out at their Christmas play. As an adult, he is surprised to see that the tormentors of his boyhood are nothing more than old men who take an almost childish delight in slipping and sliding around on the ice in the schoolyard. He has a drink and a chat with the new principal, and this clergyman is presented in a sympathetic light. However, he reveals to Jack that he never intended to become a priest but simply drifted into it as a result of being educated through school and college by the

Presentation Order. It seems that it is only when members of the clergy are not overly tied to religion that they are acceptable to the author.

The most colourful representative of old-style Catholicism in this novel is Father Creedon, or 'Credo' as he is known to the local children. He is a larger-than-life figure and a rather stereotypically strict and unforgiving priest. His role in the novel is almost theatrical: he is always shown as publicly berating members of his congregation; he throws a local drunkard out of church for misbehaviour during Mass; he throws young Jack out of the choir for having a dreadful singing voice and out of the confessional for forgetting the words of a prayer; he accosts Jack's father in the street for failing to teach his son the words of the prayer; and he is disgusted when onlookers flee in terror from the scene of an exorcism he performs. Although he is described in a very amusing way, Father Creedon is a one-dimensional character and might be seen as the author's way of expressing his distaste for the rather rigid and unforgiving attitude of the Catholic Church of the time.

Power

The power in this novel rests firmly with the wealthy, educated members of society. Jack's family is working class, and he has to decide whether to accept this position in society, like his father, or attempt to break free and make his own way in the world, untrammelled by his poor background. Unlike his father, he longs to escape the constrictions of an unfair system in which the wealthy are regarded as superior, not because they are inherently better than the poorer members of society, but because they have inherited their money and their position from their parents.

The novel is set in the thirties and forties, a time that saw a shift in the balance of power in Ireland. Prior to the War of Independence in 1922, the Anglo-Irish had been the dominant class in Ireland, but with independence came a redrawing of the lines. An example of this is to be seen in the passing of Enderley (the Jacobs' home) to a Catholic family. The name of the house is changed to Santa Maria, and the new owners, while wealthy, are representative of a newly rich social class. Unlike their predecessors, the newcomers are not used to having servants and do not treat their employees as well as the Jacob family did. They have risen in the world and are acutely aware of their roots. They are suspicious of employees like Jack's father because they think he is like them, viewing employers as foreigners and therefore cheating them at any opportunity. However, although their background may be different from the Anglo-Irish upper class who ruled the country before independence, these new employers are just as powerful and influential as those who came before them.

Marriage, family and children

Family is central to *Home Before Night*. Jack is an only child and is adored by his parents, both of whom are middle-aged when they adopt him. As he doesn't have any siblings, Jack is the entire focus of his parents' attention and they do everything they can for him.

Large families were the norm in Ireland at the time and it was difficult for working-class parents to feed, clothe and educate all their children.

> Large families were the norm in Ireland at the time and it was difficult for working-class parents to feed, clothe and educate all their children

Jack's mother was married off to his father when she was seventeen and her parents were delighted to have one less mouth to feed and to have found a man with a steady job who would be able to provide for their daughter. Her opinion was 'neither sought nor offered', and nobody cared whether or not she had any romantic feelings for Jack's father.

Jack is in a rather privileged position in that he does not have to share the family's meagre resources with any brothers or sisters. Neither is there quite the same pressure on him to leave school and go to work that there would be if he were part of a large family. The neighbouring Costellos have nine children and none of them are educated past primary school level. However, there are disadvantages too. Jack is keenly aware of the sacrifices that his parents make for him and of the hopes his mother in particular has for his future. Neither wanting nor daring to displease his mother, he acquiesces to her order to apply for a job in the civil service when he leaves school, even though it is not what he wants to do with his life. His opinion on the matter is not sought, no more than his mother's was when her parents decided to arrange her marriage to Jack's father. Jack's obedience would not be viewed as unusual at the time; it was expected that children would do what their parents told them.

The aspect of family life that causes Jack the most difficulty is the issue of his illegitimacy. His mother uses it as a weapon against him when she is angry, and as a means of gaining the sympathy and admiration of others. At that time, illegitimacy was a stigma, and Jack is embarrassed and distressed by the repeated references to his birth. Jack's mother's attitude is supported by many of those around her: her own mother, friends and even the family doctor told her that she was taking a risk by adopting a child who might prove to be unhealthy or who might turn against her.

Theme or Issue

Higher Level and Ordinary Level

Past questions on this mode of comparison have tended to focus on the following:

Higher Level

- *What insights you gained from studying the theme*
- *How the study of a particular text changed or reinforced your view of the theme*
- *The way in which key moments can heighten your awareness of a particular theme*
- *How the presentation of the theme can add to the impact of the text*
- *How the theme helps to maintain your interest in the text.*

Ordinary Level

- *What you learned about your chosen theme*
- *How a key moment in the text reveals the theme*
- *Why you feel that the theme made the text interesting*
- *How the theme is presented in the text*
- *How the theme plays an important role in the story*
- *How the theme affects the life of a character in the text.*

Theme or Issue: escape

The theme of escape is a predominant one in *Home Before Night*. As the author grows from boy to man, he is increasingly filled with a desire to escape the pressure and expectations that come with being an only child of doting parents, to leave behind the stigma of his illegitimacy, to free himself from the strictures of his social class and to avoid becoming trapped in a dead-end job.

The opening chapter introduces us to some of the members of Jack's extended family. Although they are a close family, this is more a product of circumstances than because they actively want to be together. Jack's grandmother and two of her adult children share a two-room cottage, Jack's aunt Mary sleeping in the bed with Jack's grandmother while his uncle Sonny sleeps on the settle bed in the other room. The impression we are given is of a claustrophobic, rather hopeless situation. Jack's aunt Chris is 'the success of the family' because she has managed to escape the tiny labourer's cottage and the future that awaited most girls of her class. The majority of her friends could only expect 'to become kitchen maids or dailies and to marry from one slum into the other'. Given the unappealing descriptions of the Doyles' situation, it is little wonder that Jack too should wish to avoid becoming trapped in a dead-end life.

> Given the unappealing descriptions of the Doyles' situation, it is little wonder that Jack too should wish to avoid becoming trapped in a dead-end life

Even as a very young boy, Jack is unhappily aware that he is adopted and that fact seems to haunt him, often cropping up at times of crisis, when his mother or his aunt uses the story of his birth as a way to hurt him. On a family outing around the bay, Jack's mother threatens to give him back to his birth mother if he is bold, and he is terrified at the thought. His misery is compounded by his mother's drunkenness and aggression. He is helpless and cannot do anything but stand and watch when she starts an argument with a strange man while his father attempts to calm her down. Because he is powerless to do anything practical, Jack escapes by casting his mind back to happier times and remembering another, far more pleasant family outing. However, his attempt to lose himself in the recollection of a perfect Christmas trip to Pim's is only a partial success. His escapist fantasy is destroyed when Jack is betrayed by his own imagination. In his vision, he and his mother are recognised and pointed out by people who saw her behaving badly on the cruise around Howth.

The issue of his birth continues to trouble Jack throughout his childhood. When he is very young, he finds it difficult to shake himself free of the spectre of his birth mother coming to take him away. As this fear fades, however, it is replaced by feelings of misery, resentment and embarrassment when the story of his adoption is raised. All Jack's attempts to escape the stigma associated with his illegitimacy are thwarted by his mother, who takes every opportunity to tell people she meets how she had taken in baby Jack 'when his own didn't want him'. Literature provides Jack with a way of leaving the harsher realities of his life behind, even for a short time. He loses himself in schoolboy comics like *The Magnet* and dreams of going to a school like those in the comics. When he wins the scholarship to Presentation College, it seems as if Jack's dream is about to come true and he will be able to reinvent himself. Not only will he be rising above the neighbouring children, he will also be escaping the shame of everyone knowing that he is adopted. However, Jack's hopes of becoming 'a different person' are dashed when his mother boasts to the principal of her selflessness in taking in and raising a child who was not her own.

> Jack's hopes of becoming 'a different person' are dashed when his mother boasts to the principal of her selflessness in taking in and raising a child who was not her own

Jack's years in Presentation College are not happy ones and he leaves after four years, with no Leaving Certificate and without a backward glance. A story he tells of visiting the school some years later seems to justify Jack's decision to abandon his education and get away as soon as he could. The new principal of the school confides in Jack that he is only in the priesthood because he lacked the courage to tell anyone that it was not the life he wanted. At each stage of his education and right up until the eve of his ordination, he planned to escape but never did. This is a salutary tale and its inclusion in the novel gives weight to the author's horror of being trapped in a life and a career that he does not want. He must now decide whether he will choose his own path rather than one others might choose for him, or whether he will, like the principal, put it off until it is too late.

His schooldays over, Jack is faced with the realisation that he is not much closer to escaping the confines of his family life and the limitations of his home town than he ever was. He spends much of his free time going to the cinema with his friends, watching whatever films are on, even if they are no good. The author reflects that the value of such films is that they allow him and the other boys to live 'any lives in preference to our own'. The imagery used to describe the places where the boys hang around reinforces the idea that they are stuck in a prison and are waiting to be 'set free from each other by marriage, a job, a twist of fate, a miracle'. They are 'short-term prisoners' in the 'exercise yard that is the sea-front'. There is a note of hope: the author says that very few people have ever 'served a life sentence'. Most succeed in their bid for freedom.

Jack's parents' attitude towards their son's desire to escape reflects their personalities. His mother reacts to his spending less time at home by adopting the hurt air of 'a woman whose lover has been attempting to steal off to greener pastures'. She does everything in her power to make Jack feel guilty and, while she knows that his leaving is inevitable, Jack says wryly that she will not 'lift a finger to help me cut the umbilical cord'. Jack's father, on the other hand, is as easygoing and undemanding as always, never mentioning the fact that Jack is spending less and less time at home. Jack says, 'He made it easy for me to escape, and for that reason I dawdled gratefully as one does when assured that the cell-door is open.'

> *'a woman whose lover has been attempting to steal off to greener pastures'*

The greatest obstacle to Jack's efforts to escape is his job in the civil service. In an echo of the principal who lacked the nerve to tell his parents or superiors that he did not want to become a priest, Jack finds himself giving in to his family's pressure to take the post 'because Yes was always easier to say than No'. He is not able to shake off the stigma of his illegitimacy at work either: his mother is quick to tell the whole story to Mr Drumm when he meets Jack prior to giving him a reference. Jack is sick at the thought that this tale, which he was unable to escape in school, will now follow him to this new stage in his life.

The prison metaphors continue when the author describes his time in the civil service. On his first day, he reflects bitterly that he has worn new trousers 'to go to prison'. There is a lump in his throat as he contemplates the miserable prospect of enduring the same boring job for years. 'All he could think of was escaping: soon, somehow.'

> *'All he could think of was escaping: soon, somehow'*

In the end, it is literature that shows him 'the door he would escape through'. On the recommendation of a colleague, he goes to the Abbey Theatre to see Seán O'Casey's *The Plough and the Stars* and he is swept away by the 'life that roared through the play'. He knows now that he wants to write and that this will be his route to freedom. It is fourteen years before he is established enough as a writer to afford to leave the financial security of his civil service job, but he survives by telling himself that it is not for ever, that he will succeed in carving out a new life for himself in the theatre. He is so afraid of becoming trapped in the civil service that he refuses to take any steps towards a possible promotion lest he succeeds and finds that the extra money weakens his 'resolve to be quit of the place'. Each day, as he leaves work, he feels 'like a prisoner on bail', knowing that he is only free until the next morning.

Eventually, of course, the author does escape. He leaves the civil service and he leaves Ireland, moving to London with his wife and daughter. It has taken a long time, but his efforts to gain his freedom have been largely successful. Still, even in his new life, he finds it impossible to shake off all traces of the pressure and guilt that are part and parcel of his upbringing. His mother dies and his father is clearly unable to cope alone. He refuses to join his son in London, preferring to remain at home surrounded by the memories of his late wife. Eventually, a friend of the author's phones him to say that Mr Drumm has been complaining about his father, calling him 'a public nuisance' who should be put into care. It seems that it is not as easy to get away from the negative aspects of his life as the author had hoped.

The book ends with the author's return to Ireland two years after the death of his father and Mr Drumm. He has succeeded as a writer and is following a path he has chosen for himself. The final image in the book is of the author as a young boy, hurrying towards the warmth and security of his home. This reflects the author's feelings of nostalgia and happiness as he returns home now, many years later and on his own terms. His escape is complete and there is nothing to run from any more.

Relationships

Ordinary Level **or** as a **Theme Option** for Higher Level

These notes focus on the relationship between Jack and his father. The significance of this relationship can be seen in the fact that the author also wrote a play called Da *which deals with many of the same events as those detailed in this book and focuses principally on Hugh Leonard's feelings about his father.*

However, if you wish, you may also prepare notes on the relationship between Jack and his mother or the relationship between Jack and Mr Drumm.

Past questions on Relationships (Ordinary Level) have tended to focus on the following:

- *Why you find the relationship to be complicated*
- *Why you consider the relationship to be successful*
- *Why you consider the relationship to be a failure*
- *Why the relationship made a strong impression on you.*

Jack and his father

When he is a young boy, Jack's relationship with his father is a straightforward one. They go for walks together in the evenings and his father tells him the history of the locality. They follow the same path, summer and winter, and the author describes their route and their routine in loving detail. He feels safe and secure with his father and shares the older man's pride in their home town and his joy in the beauty of the mountains and the sea.

However, even in these perfect shared times there is a hint of the change that will take place in the relationship as Jack grows up. One of the places of interest that Jack's father points out to his son is Torca Cottage on Dalkey hill, where George Bernard Shaw once lived. Jack is so used to the walk that when his father asks him who lived in that house the boy can rattle off the answer, although the name means nothing to him. On one of their strolls he asks his father who Shaw was, but his father does not give a satisfactory reply, saying merely that Shaw was 'a comical card'. Jack senses, even then, that his father doesn't give a proper answer because he doesn't know much, if anything, about Shaw. While his father's lack of education does not trouble young Jack, it becomes more of an issue as he grows older and the gap between his father's knowledge and his own widens.

The perfection of the walk is slightly marred on one occasion when Jack's father tells his son the story of Old Higgins, a godless man who is buried on the hill they're standing on and who is reputed to have been carried off by the devil. Jack is appalled at the thought of Higgins's ghost lurking on the hill, and insists that they go straight home. He clutches his father's trouser pocket as they walk and, prompted by the terrifying story of Old Higgins, admits that there is another story that frightens him even more; he is dreadfully afraid that his birth mother will appear one day and take him away. His parents had reassured him with a false tale of his mother being stuck on Lambay Island out in the Irish Sea, but his aunt Chris had told him that this is not true. She invented a different story about his birth mother, saying that she was a tall, pale figure in a black coat who came and looked through the window at him at night. Jack's father admits that Jack's birth mother does not live on Lambay Island and says that Jack is now old enough to know the truth, claiming that the woman actually lives on the Kish lightship. Young Jack, still at an age where he believes everything he is told, is vastly relieved and is filled with love and admiration for his father. His joy is compounded when his father assures him that, should his real mother ever turn up at their house, he will come up behind her and 'give her the biggest root up the arse a

Young Jack, still at an age where he believes everything he is told, is vastly relieved and is filled with love and admiration for his father woman ever got'. Moved almost to tears of gratitude, Jack reflects that his father is 'the best da in the whole of Dalkey'. This moment is significant in that it shows Jack's father's love for his son and his desire to keep him happy and safe. However, the story he makes up to quell the boy's fears is not one that will stand the test of time. Just as Jack outgrew his belief that his mother lived on Lambay Island, so he will outgrow this new tale. Jack's father's solutions to life's problems are simplistic and it is inevitable that his son will reach a stage where he is no longer comforted by fairytales and brave promises to give those who upset him a kick in the seat of the pants.

For his part, Jack's father accepts his son's love with his usual easygoing, positive, uncomplicated approach to life. As they stroll down the hill to the town, Jack catches hold of his father's hand and says, 'Da, I love you.' His father's reply, 'Certainly you do. Why wouldn't you?' is touching as it shows his unquestioning acceptance of this happy relationship. It never seems to occur to him that there is another option and that he and his son might not always be this close.

As Jack nears adolescence, his relationship with his father goes through a transitional phase. He still respects and admires his father, but he has come to accept that he does not have all the answers. However, when Jack needs to know the meaning of the word 'adultery', he is forced to turn to him, having been severely punished for asking the same question in school. This is a desperate measure; Jack admits that 'the last person I would normally ask for information or advice was my father'. As it happens, his father confuses the word 'adultery' with 'dilution'. He half fills a cup with milk, then tops it up with water and announces triumphantly that the resulting liquid is an example of adultery. Jack is old enough to know that his father's knowledge is limited, but still young enough to take his word on certain matters, so he is satisfied with this explanation.

'the last person I would normally ask for information or advice was my father'

When Jack was a very young boy, he believed that his father was 'the best da in the whole of Dalkey'. Dalkey was his universe and he knew nothing of the world beyond it. As he grows older, however, his horizons expand and with this new knowledge of the world comes the realisation of his father's limitations. Jack is torn between loving his father and being proud of the work he does to provide for his family, and feeling ashamed of his obvious poverty and lack of sophistication. When Jack starts in Presentation College, he is desperate to fit in with the middle-class boys and is therefore horrified when his father insists on accompanying him to the school on his first day. The other boys spot Jack's father at the gate and sneer at the 'quaint old gentleman'. Jack is overcome by 'the shame and the shame of being ashamed' and punches one of the jeering boys in the face. The mixture of emotions Jack feels at this moment encapsulates his mixed feelings towards his father. He dislikes the disloyalty he sees in himself when he tries to deny his background, particularly as his father is willing to give all he has to his son to give him every chance to get on in life. Ironically, the better educated Jack becomes and the more he learns of the world, the wider the gap between himself and his father becomes.

It is not just the boys in Presentation College who draw Jack's attention to his father's shortcomings. His mother is also well aware that her husband can appear foolish when he holds forth with his ill-formed opinions on serious matters. For this reason, she instructs Jack's father to hold his tongue when Mr Drumm visits the house to meet Jack prior to giving him a reference for the civil service. Jack's father, 'not able to sit quiet if it killed him', ignores her and embarrasses Jack with his confidently expressed but naive political views. When they are alone together later, Mr Drumm reinforces Jack's impression of his father as a rather ridiculous figure by describing him as 'inoffensive, stupid and not a damn bit of good'. As Mr Drumm is a respectable man from a slightly higher social class than Jack's parents, his words carry weight. Mr Drumm admits to having 'a fondness' for Jack's father, but only because he is amusing and hard-working. However, the overall impression he gives Jack is that he would do better in life if he were to distance himself from his father and those like him.

Although Jack's view of his father may be changing as he grows up, Jack's father still loves his son in the same unconditional, unquestioning way he always did. He appears blithely unaware that his behaviour might be embarrassing at times or that Jack is slowly drifting away from him. He continues to do his best for his son and Jack feels increasingly guilty as he sees how hard his father works to provide for the family. Believing that Jack must have a new suit for his interview with the civil service, Jack's father takes on a second job to earn the necessary money. He comes home exhausted each evening and Jack feels guilty that he should be the cause of his father's tiredness. Angrily, he says he does not want the money and tries to make his father spend it on himself, but his father is bewildered at the suggestion, claiming that he and Jack's mother are perfectly well-situated and 'wantin' nothin' from no one'.

Jack's father does not demand any more of Jack than he does of his employers or anyone else in his life, and Jack is grateful for this when the time comes for him to pull away from his parents and start to live a more independent life. His father accepts that Jack spends less and less time with his family and more time with his friends 'with the unconcern of a fancier releasing a pigeon that he knows will fly home'.

> *'with the unconcern of a fancier releasing a pigeon that he knows will fly home'*

Because Jack's father makes it easy for his son to escape, Jack does not feel under pressure to fight for his freedom in the same way that he does when he is dealing with his mother. Whether it is deliberate or not, Jack's father's handling of his son's growing independence strengthens the father–son relationship.

Jack does gain his longed-for independence, but with this comes an increased distance between himself and his father. Gone are the days of walks together around Dalkey and family outings to the cinema. The last trip Jack and his father take together is on the final tram from Dalkey to the city centre. The author names all the places they pass on their journey, as he did on those evening walks with his father long ago. The ending of the tram service symbolises the ending of an era. Jack is an adult now, and although he loves his father still, he is moving on with his own life.

Jack emigrates to England with his wife and child and therefore sees less of his father. When Jack's mother dies, his father begins to slide into senility. He refuses Jack's offer to take him to London to live with him, insisting that he can take care of himself. This is an awkward stage in the relationship between father and son. Jack is clearly uncomfortable with his father's decision and feels guilty for not forcing the issue. For his part, Jack's father believes he is putting no pressure on his son to do anything for him by claiming that he is more than capable of coping alone. He is not, and Jack is aware of the fact. When a friend phones him to say that Mr Drumm has been complaining about his father's erratic behaviour and saying that he should be put in care, Jack is furious, partly because he knows Mr Drumm is right and that he must face the fact that the old man can no longer care for himself. Jack's father is first placed in an institution that is a cross between a nursing home and a hospital, and then, when his condition deteriorates, in a psychiatric hospital. Jack is not with him when he dies, but he draws some consolation from the fact that his father died peacefully.

Two years after his father's death, Jack returns to Ireland for good. As he drives towards Dublin, he remembers 'another journey home, long ago'. He recalls a time when, as a small boy of seven or eight, he had stayed out late one autumn afternoon,

'the two lighted rooms that were the harbour at the world's end'

unaware that the light was fading as evening fell. The author's final memory in the novel is of this childhood version of himself running home as fast as he can, towards his waiting parents and the safety of his home: 'the two lighted rooms that were the harbour at the world's end'. In his mind's eye, his father is anxiously studying the clock, wondering why his son isn't home yet. This touching, affectionate recollection sets the seal on the author's fond memories of his childhood and of his loving relationship with his father.

Hero/Heroine/Villain

Ordinary Level

Note

In this mode, students may choose a hero **or** heroine **or** villain from their Comparative Study texts.

Past questions on this mode of comparison have tended to focus on the following:
- *Why you find the hero/heroine/villain interesting*
- *Why you consider the character to be a hero/heroine/villain*
- *What part the hero/heroine/villain plays in the storyline.*

Hero

Jack is the hero of *Home Before Night*. As this is an autobiographical novel, Jack is central to the text and we follow his progress through childhood, adolescence and early adulthood. He is an appealing character and it is easy to relate to him as he shares his hopes, fears, frustrations and joy with the reader.

One of the aspects of the text which helps us to identify with Jack is the switching between first and third person narration. The second chapter is narrated from the point of view of the author as a young boy helplessly watching his mother's unpleasant, drunken behaviour on a family outing. The simple language and the lack of adult analysis of the events highlight the way this day would have appeared to a small child. The effect of this is to draw us in to the little boy's world and it would be almost impossible not to empathise with Jack's misery on the train journey as, unnoticed by his mother, he retrieves his torn comic from her and reflects that there will be 'time enough for a cry' later on when he is safely home.

When chapters are narrated in the first person, we share Jack's adult version of significant moments in his life. He is witty, humorous and admirably self-deprecating in his accounts of his schooldays, his adolescence and his years of drudgery in the civil service. It is the author's honesty and acceptance of his own role in the failures and disappointments he encountered that make him a hero we respect. For example, his time in Presentation College is a deeply unhappy one, but the author admits that part of the reason he was bullied by a small gang of boys who mocked his poor background was that 'my own snobbery was fuel for theirs'. He knows now that being ashamed of his family's poverty unwittingly encouraged others to mock him for it.

As a young boy, Jack wants to be a hero but he never quite succeeds. He longs to be like one of the 'Chaps' in the stories he reads about English public schoolboys. The cinema fuels this desire to be a hero, but Jack seems doomed to failure in his efforts to live up to his ideal. A primary school teacher punishes him for inadvertently dirtying his copybook with ink, and Jack reflects sadly that 'the more he wanted to be like the Chap in the serial at the Picture House, the more people kept treating him like the Bully instead'. Secondary school is worse; not only does Jack fall out with the popular boys when he punches the fellow who jeers at his father's poverty, but he is sidelined when raffle tickets are handed out for sale on his first day. The principal is worried that Jack might steal the money because he is from a working-class background. Jack feels that his dream of being a paragon of schoolboy virtue will never be realised. Although he may not be the Chap he had hoped to become, we admire him for his dreams and for his openness in admitting his failure to achieve his ambition.

'the more he wanted to be like the Chap in the serial at the Picture House, the more people kept treating him like the Bully instead'

On other occasions, Jack can be a genuine bully rather than being cast in that role by others. He uses his quick wit and sharp tongue to make a fool of Tommy Martin, a harmless middle-aged man who likes to hang around with him and his friends. We forgive him his cruelty because he has learned a lesson from it and says that his friends, who had 'an in-bred tact and tolerance that I lacked', left the older man alone. Jack is not perfect, but human faults and failings can make a hero more appealing to the reader, particularly when, as in Jack's case, that character shows that he has gained from the experience and is likely to become a better person as a result.

> Jack's relationship with his parents is not always an easy one, but he is a loyal and loving son

Jack's relationship with his parents is not always an easy one, but he is a loyal and loving son. He appreciates the sacrifices they make for him and he knows how hard his father works to provide for his family. When Jack's father uncomplainingly takes on extra work so that he can afford to buy Jack a suit for his civil service interview, Jack tells him to spend the money on himself. His father doesn't (it would not be in his nature), but we admire Jack for the concern he shows for his father, who comes home exhausted every night.

As he grows older, Jack replaces his old dream of being a Chap with a new dream: to break away from his working-class background and to seek a better life than that of his parents and neighbours. He faces many obstacles as he sets out to achieve this goal, but he does ultimately succeed. His mother is a powerfully antagonistic force in his struggle to break free. Jack says that she would not 'lift a finger to help me cut the umbilical cord'. It is she who, aided and abetted by her sister Chris, pressurises Jack into joining the civil service. His resolve falters in the face of her determination and, 'because Yes was always easier to say than No', he takes the job. This is a serious setback in Jack's plan to lead a life of his own choosing but he freely admits that the fault is his. He should have stood up for himself and his failure to do so makes him miserable. Still, he does not abandon his ambition and we respect his refusal to allow himself to be promoted in the service, lest it corrupt his resolve 'to be quit of the place'.

By the final chapter of the novel we are totally immersed in Jack's story. We know how much he loathes his job in the civil service and we share in his delight when he becomes a successful enough writer to resign from his detested position in the Land Commission. This is not quite a happy ever afterwards, however. Although he moves to London with his wife and daughter, Jack has to cope with the fact that his father, who stubbornly insists on remaining at home rather than moving to England with his son, is failing mentally and physically. We can relate to Jack's mixed feelings of love, frustration, sorrow and guilt as his father's condition deteriorates and he eventually dies in a psychiatric hospital.

Our final impression of Jack is a positive one. He has come a long way in life. He has achieved his ambition of becoming a professional writer and escaping the restrictions of a job he hated. Now he can return to the place where he grew up, but on his own terms. As he drives towards Dublin city, he reflects nostalgically on another journey home, many years ago. He thinks affectionately of the warmth and welcome that awaited him in his family home.

Jack is not a perfect character, but his honesty, decency, humour and refusal to allow his dream to die make him a hero whose adventures we are happy to share.

Aspects of Story: Tension, Climax or Resolution

Ordinary Level

Past questions on this mode of comparison have tended to focus on the following:

- *How does the tension **or** climax **or** resolution hold your interest in the story being told?*
- *What is the importance of the tension **or** climax **or** resolution in the text?*
- *Discuss a key moment in which the tension **or** climax **or** resolution is clearly shown.*

Tension

It might seem, at first glance, that an autobiographical account of the author's early life in Dublin is not a subject likely to generate much tension, but Hugh Leonard's storytelling is so amusing and the characters he describes so engaging that the reader is soon engrossed in these warm, witty memoirs.

One of the ways in which the author captures our attention and makes us want to read on is his use of dramatic opening or closing lines in many of the chapters. For example, the first sentence in the book is: 'My grandmother made dying her life's work.' It would be an unusual reader who did not wish to find out what exactly the author meant by this astonishing statement. The final sentence in the first chapter is no less intriguing. Having just told us that his aunt Chris remained childless, the author goes on to tell us: 'For that matter, none of the Doyles of Chris's generation had children – including my mother.' The casual way this comment is made does not diminish the tension it creates and we are compelled to read on to discover how this apparent contradiction will be explained.

In the second chapter, the narration moves from first to third person. The story of a family outing ruined by Jack's mother's drunken unpleasantness is told from the point of view of seven- or eight-year-old Jack. This adds greatly to the tension of the story as we see events unfolding from the perspective of a small boy, distressed and embarrassed by his mother's behaviour. On the train ride back to Dalkey, Jack reflects on what is likely to happen when he gets home. He seems sure that his mother will start a row and he tells us: 'He would back-answer her and the day would end with a slap and the hard feel of her ring.' There is a note of resignation in his use of the conditional tense ('would back-answer', 'would end') when he describes this scenario. It tells the reader that the boy is accustomed to such treatment when his mother has drink taken.

'He would back-answer her and the day would end with a slap and the hard feel of her ring'

Jack's journey through childhood, adolescence and early adulthood is not a particularly unusual one. Like most people, he has ups and downs with family and friends and struggles to find his own identity and independence as he grows older. But instead of making the text less interesting, the familiarity of these tales of tension between parents and child, conflict between schoolchildren, unkind teachers and unfair employers draw us in because we can relate to them.

Jack has to wrestle with two demons: the stigma of his illegitimacy and his fear of being trapped for ever in a life like his father's. The issue of his birth is raised in Chapter 2 when Jack's mother tells strangers on the train that he was 'a nurse-child', and it recurs as a cause of great tension between Jack and his mother throughout the novel. The drudgery of Jack's father's job, working as a gardener seven days a week for fifty-four years, has instilled in young Jack a horror of ending up in a similar position. He is torn between love for his father and frustration that he sees nothing wrong with his life. In order to get away from unpleasant realities, even for a while, Jack loses himself in comic book stories of British public schoolboys and in films featuring dashing heroes. His dream is to become like them.

When Jack is offered a scholarship to secondary school, it seems that his dream of bettering himself is about to come true and he will at last be like one of the Chaps in *The Magnet* comic. He and his mother go to see Brother Berchmans, the principal of Presentation College. The description of Brother Berchmans does not bode well for Jack's future happiness in the school and immediately introduces a note of tension. He is described as having 'eyes like the sea in March' and his robes hiss 'like snakes' as he walks. His voice hints at menace too: his words are cut short 'as if with a nail scissors'.

Jack seems oblivious to any possible problems and waits happily outside the principal's office while his mother goes inside for what Brother Berchmans calls 'a privvit word'. The third person narration in this section shows us Jack's innocence and vulnerability by allowing us to see the events unfold from the perspective of a young boy sitting in a chair that is too big for him, swinging his legs and banging his fists on his knees 'with the excitement of being in Presentation'. He imagines himself talking like his schoolboy heroes in *The Magnet*, calling out, 'I say, you chaps!' and similar expressions associated with the English upper class. We are aware, though young Jack is not, that the boys in Presentation College are highly unlikely to speak this way, and we feel anxious for Jack because he seems ill-prepared for the reality of secondary school. The way he expresses his delight ('Jasus, it would be great') serves to highlight the distance between Jack's situation and the social class to which he aspires. Not only would the boys in *The Magnet* never say 'Jasus', neither would the middle-class boys in Presentation College.

Our concern for Jack deepens when we learn that his mother has told Brother Berchmans all about his adoption. Jack's heart sinks at the thought that the other boys will find out, but he consoles himself with the thought that Brother Berchmans, like the teachers in *The Magnet*, will be strict but fair, and will keep Jack's secret to himself. However, as he goes on to share stories of his education to date, we realise that

> we feel anxious for Jack because he seems ill-prepared for the reality of secondary school

schooling in Ireland at the time is far from the ideal Jack dreams of. It seems more likely that the teachers in Presentation College will be little different from those he has had in his previous schools. This turns out to be the case and Jack's first day in Presentation College puts an end to all his hopes of shaking off his past and reinventing himself. His fight with the boys who mock his father's shabby appearance, and Brother Berchmans' refusal to allow him to sell raffle tickets lest he steal the money, show that we had good cause to feel anxious on Jack's behalf when he went to that first meeting.

As Jack reaches the end of his miserable career in Presentation College, we wonder once again what the future holds for him. He has no qualifications, is leaving school without a Leaving Certificate, and the prospect of his ending up in a menial job like his father's seems more likely than ever, adding to the tension of the story. We know that being trapped in a dead-end job is something Jack dreads but we cannot see what else lies in store for him.

> We know that being trapped in a dead-end job is something Jack dreads but we cannot see what else lies in store for him

The tension of Jack's situation is shown in the way he describes his life. For example, he and his friends spend their free time at the seafront, a place Jack compares to a prison from which they are waiting to be set free. They console themselves with the knowledge that most people do get away and that this prison is only 'for short-term prisoners'. We wonder how Jack will effect this escape as he does not appear to have any real plan for his future.

Climax

The moment of greatest tension in Jack's story occurs when he gives in to his mother's and aunt's wish that he join the civil service. That this decision is a mistake is obvious from the moment Mr Drumm comes to the Keyes' house to meet Jack prior to giving him a reference. In the same way that the menace of Brother Berchmans was signalled by the description of his appearance and mannerisms, so Mr Drumm is presented as a forbidding and intimidating character. He is 'thin and stiff as a hatstand' and his lips are 'as thin as Lent'. He speaks curtly to Jack's mother, calling her 'a foolish woman' for offering him a cup of tea. Tea is a scarce commodity during wartime, but Mr Drumm's reprimand is both ungrateful and condescending. He is no more friendly in his dealings with Jack, pulling him up for saying 'yeah' instead of 'yes'. Mr Drumm goes on to advise Jack against joining the civil service, saying that he regrets ever having taken a position there himself. His words reinforce Jack's fears and add to the feeling of hopelessness and despair that mark this moment in his life.

Just when it appears that things could not get any worse for Jack, they do. He overhears his mother telling Mr Drumm the story of his adoption and he walks out into the garden, sick at the thought that the story he detests will follow him into the civil service, just as it followed him into Presentation College. The weather reflects Jack's mood: 'cold needles of rain' drop on him as he waits for Mr Drumm to emerge from the house. Mr Drumm and Jack talk privately in the pub and the conversation gives Jack no reason to view his future in a more positive light. The civil service, claims Mr Drumm, is 'like a lobster pot, harder to get out of than into'. He warns Jack that he is throwing his life away, a fact Jack is already keenly aware of.

As well as voicing Jack's fear that he is about to be trapped in a job he will hate, Mr Drumm brings up the other issue which has plagued Jack's life: the fact that he is adopted. Mr Drumm does so harshly, referring to Jack as 'illegitimate' and his situation as 'bastardy', words that bring tears to Jack's eyes. Mr Drumm is unrepentant and goes on to give his opinion of Jack's father, calling him the sort of man who is 'inoffensive, stupid and not a damn bit of good'. It seems that Mr Drumm is determined to make Jack face all the unpleasant realities of his life: a job he will hate, an ignorant father, and illegitimacy.

'inoffensive, stupid and not a damn bit of good'

The meeting with Mr Drumm marks the beginning of the lowest point of Jack's life. The civil service is all Jack feared it might be. He is placed in Mr Drumm's section and has to endure his superior's disapproval and dislike when they fall out for a reason which is never entirely clear to Jack. Mr Drumm is only part of the reason Jack is unhappy in his job. His heart sinks at the thought that he will have to 'climb the same stairs forever to sit and write Receivable Orders'. The first day passes slowly and Jack reflects bitterly that he has worn new trousers 'to go to prison'. He is consumed by the thought of escape, but cannot see how this could be achieved. His situation appears hopeless.

Resolution

Jack's salvation comes unexpectedly, six months or so after he starts his new job. He is whistling a tune at his desk one day when a colleague remarks that that tune features in *The Plough and the Stars*. Jack has never heard of the play and the other man advises him to go and see it as soon as possible. He knows that Jack wants to be a writer and he says that, by not knowing such an important play, Jack is 'making a holy show' of himself. His advice is kindly and well-meant, and Jack decides to act on it. He goes to the Abbey Theatre that very evening and sees a professionally staged play for the first time. His life is changed utterly by his trip to the theatre. Now he knows with a burning clarity that he wants to be a playwright. He will 'never again be content just to sit and watch and applaud like the rest of them'. Jack has at last found the door through which he will escape.

> His life is changed utterly by his trip to the theatre. Now he knows with a burning clarity that he wants to be a playwright

Fortunately for Jack's peace of mind, he does not know that it will take him a full fourteen years to get away from the civil service. But his job seems less oppressive now that he is working towards an aim and believes the end is in sight. He joins the dramatic society and starts writing plays of his own.

Jack's uneasy relationship with Mr Drumm is never fully resolved, although they do part on good terms when Jack leaves the civil service to write full time. To Jack's surprise, Mr Drumm appears quite emotional about his departure, bemoaning the fact that he knew nothing about it until that moment and wishing Jack all the best in his future career. They meet again six years later when Jack comes home from England for his mother's funeral. He calls to Mr Drumm's house and they have a pleasant time together. In a gesture of friendship, Jack sends Mr Drumm tickets to one of his plays. To his amused irritation, Mr Drumm responds with 'a formal and detailed critique of the play'. It is easy to understand why Jack calls him 'an impossible man'. This is not the end of the connection between Jack and Mr Drumm. When Jack's father begins to grow senile, Jack hears from a friend that Mr Drumm is complaining about him and saying that he should be put into care. Jack is furious, partly because he cannot seem to get Mr Drumm out of his life and partly because he knows Mr Drumm is right. Jack's father is incapable of living alone now and Jack feels guilty that he cannot do more to help. The situation is resolved, sadly, by his father's death. Later that year, Mr Drumm dies too, 'almost as if contented that he had outlived his rival'.

Two years after his father's death, Jack returns home to Ireland to live. The final memory he shares with us, as he drives back towards Dublin, is of another journey home, long ago. He remembers an evening when he was seven or eight and was hurrying home, having stayed out until close to nightfall. He sees himself as a young boy, running as fast as possible towards the warmth and welcome of 'the two lighted rooms that were the harbour at world's end'. This charming, uplifting image shows us that Jack has moved beyond seeing his home place as a restrictive influence on his life and that he is now in a position to view his family with love and understanding. Home is no longer a place to run from, but a place to run to.

> Home is no longer a place to run from, but a place to run to

glossary

Assegai:	wooden spear or javelin with a metal tip
Baby Power:	miniature bottle of Powers whiskey
Bendigo Plug:	type of tobacco
Benediction:	benediction of the Blessed Sacrament, a religious ceremony
Benison:	blessing
B and I:	British and Irish Steam Packet Company (known as the B&I) – a ferry company that ran ships between Ireland and the UK. It later became Irish Ferries
Black and Tans:	see the notes on historical background at the start of the book
Blessed Oliver Plunkett:	Irish Roman Catholic martyr and later a saint, executed in London in 1681
Chauffeuse:	female chauffeur, driver
Child of Mary:	member of a Roman Catholic society which has a special devotion to the Blessed Virgin Mary
Church of Ireland:	Anglican Church. In *Home Before Night*, the worst thing Sonny can discover about John Bennett, his future brother-in-law, is that he had a cousin who left the Roman Catholic Church to join the Church of Ireland
Codology:	nonsense, foolish behaviour, bluffing
Colloguing:	chatting with friends
Couturière:	woman who makes and/or sells designer clothes
Crony:	friend
Descartes:	René Descartes was a seventeenth-century French philosopher, mathematician and writer. His surname is pronounced, roughly,

· ·

'day cart' which is why Oliver's pronunciation of it as 'Des Carty' is held up to ridicule

Diddlum society: informal savings scheme run by a respectable, trusted local person. People would pay a certain amount of money into the society on a regular basis and they would receive their payout at Christmas

Dray-horse: draught horse used to pull heavy loads

Eucharistic Congress: large religious gathering of people to bear witness to the presence of Jesus in the Eucharist. There were international Eucharistic Congresses in Ireland in 1932 and 2012

Excoriation: hurtful or brutal criticism

Forenest: in this book, means 'sitting in front of'

Furry Glen: woodland walkway centred on a small lake in the Phoenix Park. There is no charge to walk in the Furry Glen, while there is a charge to enter the zoo

George V: King of England from 1910 to 1936

Gett: slang word meaning the same thing as 'git'; a deeply unpleasant person

Glauber salts: laxative

Go-boy: boy who acts foolishly, a 'messer'

Gostering: gossiping

Greyfriars: Greyfriars School is a fictional English school which was the setting for a series of stories that appeared in *The Magnet* from 1908 to 1940

Hansom cab:	horse-drawn cart; offered for hire in the same way as a taxi nowadays
Hobnailed:	refers to hobnailed boots (boots with nails in the soles), a common way of making cheap boots stronger and longer lasting
Horny cobbler:	colloquial term for a variety of scorpion fish caught in Irish waters. It is a small fish covered with sharp spines. In *Home Before Night* there is a reference to Jack's birth mother living on Lambay Island or the Kish Lightship and cooking pollock and horny cobblers. Both fish would have been regarded as cheap and rather unappetising food
Huxter's shop:	small, rather chaotic shop selling all sorts of cheap odds and ends
Jackeen:	derogatory term for someone from Dublin city
Jennet:	donkey mare
Kaiser:	refers to Kaiser Wilhelm II, Emperor of Germany from 1888 to 1918
Kish lightship:	a ship used as a lighthouse from 1811 to 1965. It warned sailors of the presence of the Kish Bank, a shallow sandbank about seven miles off the Dublin coast
Lambay Island:	small island off the Dublin coast
Lee Enfield:	rifle used by the British military during the first half of the twentieth century
Lèse-majesté:	treason
Lubricious:	shifty, sneaky or tricky, underhand behaviour
Marquess of Queensberry rules:	code of rules governing boxing
Men's Sodality:	Roman Catholic society which has a special devotion to the Blessed Virgin Mary
Micawber, Mr:	character in Charles Dickens' *David Copperfield*
Milliner:	maker of hats
Mitcher:	someone who skips school without permission
Nabob:	European who made a fortune in India, a wealthy, important person
Nurse-child:	illegitimate child being raised by someone other than his/her parents

Perfunctory:	done as a matter of routine, with little care or interest
Pim's:	a department store
Pig's back:	to be on the pig's back means to be very happy, content or fortunate
Oleograph:	cheap reproduction of an oil painting
Quakers:	members of the Religious Society of Friends, a Christian denomination
Quality:	people from the upper or upper middle class
Sandhurst:	military academy where British officers are trained
Seamstress:	woman who makes her living by sewing
Sedan chair:	covered seat on two poles, used to carry an important person
Settle bed:	a bed that can be folded up to become a wooden seat by day
Seven Churches:	visiting seven churches on the Thursday before Easter Sunday is an old Roman Catholic tradition
Shirtwaist:	simple dress, the upper half of which resembles a man's shirt
Sleeveen:	sneaky, untrustworthy person
Spats:	footwear accessory, worn over men's shoes and covering the instep and ankle, associated with well-off gentlemen
Spittoon:	receptacle for spitting into, particularly after chewing tobacco
Suppé:	Franz von Suppé (1819–1895) was an Austrian composer of light operas
Sweep:	the Sweepstakes – a lottery
Switzer's:	a department store
Taffeta:	light fabric used mainly for making women's dresses
Tick:	to buy something on tick is to buy it on credit. Before credit cards, this was a common enough arrangement between shops and customers. The amount owed was recorded by the shop and the buyer paid the money back at a time agreed between him or her and the shopkeeper
Ulagoning:	moaning or complaining
Via Dolorosa:	the route that Jesus followed from his condemnation by Pilate to the place of his crucifixion and thus a difficult or torturous journey/experience

nifty **notes**

FOR LEAVING CERTIFICATE ENGLISH TEXTS
ORDINARY AND HIGHER LEVEL

Other titles available in the series

How Many Miles to Babylon?
by Jennifer Johnston

Sive
by John B. Keane

educate.ie
Castleisland, Co. Kerry, Ireland
www.educate.ie